ST. MARY'S COLLEGE
LIBRARY

V. S. NAIPAUL

V. S. NAIPAUL

V. S. NAIPAUL

SUMAN GUPTA

Northcote House
in association with the
British Council

© Copyright 1999 by Suman Gupta

First published in 1999 by Northcote House Publishers Ltd, Plymbridge House, Estover Road, Plymouth PL6 7PY, United Kingdom.
Tel: +44 (01752) 202368 Fax: +44 (01752) 202330.

British Library Cataloguing-in-Publication Data
A catalogue record for this book is available from the British Library

ISBN 0-7463-0897-3

Typeset by PDQ Typesetting, Newcastle-under-Lyme
Printed and bound in the United Kingdom

Dedicated to my parents

Contents

Acknowledgements

Thanks are due to Maya Gupta for helping me find some of Naipaul's recent articles and interviews which were published in India. I am grateful to Erik Svarny and Subarno Chattarji for going through a first draft of the manuscript and making some necessary changes and useful suggestions. Any errors and defects that remain are entirely my responsibility. I would also like to take this opportunity to express my gratitude to my wife, Cheng, and our son, Ayan, for their support.

Biographical Outline

1932   Vidiadhar Surajprasad Naipaul born at Chaguanas, central Trinidad, on 17 August to Seepersad Naipaul and Bropatie Naipaul (née Capildeo).

1936   Enters Chaguanas Government School.

1938   Family moves to Port of Spain. (Between 1938 and 1947 Naipaul's family moved several times: to Diego Martin in 1940, to Port of Spain again in 1941; and finally to a house of their own in Nepaul Street, St James, in 1947.) Naipaul transfers to Tranquility Boys' School.

1942   Naipaul wins an exhibition from Tranquility School (he came third in the island) and is given a free place in Queens Royal College.

1943–9   From January 1943 to April 1949, attends Queens Royal College, specializing in French and Spanish. Awarded Trinidad Government Scholarship in 1948.

1950   Returns to Queens Royal College in January as a student teacher. Works briefly in the Registrar-General's Department in the Red House, Port of Spain. Leaves on 2 August to study English literature at University College, Oxford. Starts writing occasional pieces for the BBC World Service *Caribbean Voices*.

1953   Is awarded BA (Hons.) in English.

1954   Works briefly in the Cataloguing Department of National Portrait Gallery. Becomes Editor of BBC *Caribbean Voices* programme.

1955   Marries Patricia Ann Hale.

1956   Revisits Trinidad.

1957   *The Mystic Masseur* published. Works for ten weeks at a copywriting job with a cement firm.

1958   *The Suffrage of Elvira* published. *The Mystic Masseur* awarded John Llewellyn Rhys Memorial Prize. Begins to write reviews for the *New Statesman*.

1959   *Miguel Street* published.

1960   Given a three-month fellowship by the government of Trinidad and Tobago to write on the Caribbean. Spends seven months travelling in the West Indies.

1961   *A House for Mr Biswas* appears. Awarded the Somerset Maugham Award for *Miguel Street*.

1962   *The Middle Passage* published. Leaves on his first visit to India, after being given a Phoenix Trust Award to enable him to write a book on India.

1963   *Mr Stone and the Knights Companion* published.

1964   *An Area of Darkness* appears. Awarded Hawthornden Prize for *Mr Stone and the Knights Companion*.

1965   Becomes Writer-in-residence at Makarere University, Uganda.

1966   Travels to East and Central Africa.

1967   *The Mimic Men* and *A Flag on the Island* published.

1968   Awarded W. H. Smith prize for *The Mimic Men*. Revisits Trinidad.

1969   *The Loss of El Dorado* appears. Gets Arts Council Grant to travel in the United States and Canada.

1970   Settles in Wiltshire, England.

1971   *In a Free State* published. Awarded Booker Prize for *In a Free State*. Travels in India, Mauritius, East Africa and South America. Revisits Trinidad.

1972   *The Overcrowded Barracoon* published.

1973   Goes to Trinidad to research Christina Gardens killings.

1975   *Guerrillas* appears. DLitt from University of West Indies, St Augustine Campus. Visits India.

1977   *India: A Wounded Civilization* published.

1978   Teaches in Wesleyan College, Connecticut, USA.

1979   *A Bend in the River* appears. Nominated for Booker Prize. Travels in Islamic countries.

1980   'The Return of Eva Perón' with 'The Killings in Trinidad' appears. Awarded the Bennet Award.

1981   *Among the Believers* published. Awarded Hon. Dr Letters from Columbia University, New York.

1983   Awarded the Jerusalem Prize. Awarded Hon. Litt.D., Cambridge University.

1984   *Finding the Centre* published.

1986	Wins the T. S. Eliot Award.
1988	Travels through south-eastern United States. Awarded Hon. D.Litt., London University.
1989	*A Turn in the South* appears.
1990	*India: A Million Mutinies Now* appears. Is knighted. Awarded the Trinity Cross, Trinidad.
1992	Awarded Hon. D.Litt., Oxford University.
1993	Given British Literature Prize.
1994	Naipaul archives opens at the University of Tulsa, Oklahoma, MacFarlin Library. *A Way in the World* is published.
1995	Visits Iran, Pakistan, Malaysia, and Indonesia again.
1996	First wife, Patricia Ann Hale, dies. Marries Nadira Khannum Alvi.
1998	*Beyond Belief* published.

Abbreviations and References

AB   *Among the Believers: An Islamic Journey* (London: André Deutsch, 1981)

AD   *An Area of Darkness* (1964; repr. Harmondsworth: Penguin, 1968)

BB   *Beyond Belief: Islamic Excursions Among the Converted Peoples* (London: Little, Brown, 1998)

BR   *A Bend in the River* (1979; repr. Harmondsworth: Penguin, 1980)

CD   *A Congo Diary* (Los Angeles: Sylvester and Orphanos, 1980)

EA   *The Enigma of Arrival: A Novel* (1987; repr. Harmondsworth: Penguin, 1988)

FC   *Finding the Centre: Two Narratives* (London: André Deutsch, 1984)

FI   *A Flag on the Island* (1967; repr. Harmondsworth: Penguin, 1969)

FS   *In a Free State* (1971; repr. Harmondsworth: Penguin, 1973)

G   *Guerrillas* (1975; repr. Harmondsworth: Penguin, 1976)

HB   *A House for Mr Biswas* (1961; repr. Harmondsworth: Penguin, 1969)

LED   *The Loss of El Dorado: A History* (1969; repr. Harmondsworth: Penguin, 1973)

MiM   *The Mimic Men* (1967; repr. Harmondsworth: Penguin, 1969)

MM   *The Mystic Masseur* (1957; repr. Harmondsworth: Penguin, 1969)

MMN   *India: A Million Mutinies Now* (1990; repr. London: Minerva, 1991)

MP   *The Middle Passage: Impressions of Five Societies – British, French and Dutch – in the West Indies and South America* (Harmondsworth: Penguin, 1969)

MS   *Miguel Street* (1959; repr. Harmondsworth: Penguin, 1971)

OB   *The Overcrowded Barracoon and Other Articles* (London: André Deutsch, 1972)

REP   *'The Return of Eva Perón' with 'The Killings in Trinidad'* (London: André Deutsch, 1980)

SE   *The Suffrage of Elvira* (1958; repr. London: André Deutsch [Russell Edition], 1964)

SKC   *Mr Stone and the Knights Companion* (1963; repr. Harmondsworth: Penguin, 1969)

TS   *A Turn in the South* (London: Viking, 1989)

WC   *India: A Wounded Civilization* (London: André Deutsch, 1977)

WW   *A Way in the World: A Sequence* (London: Heinemann, 1994)

1

Introduction

When asked in an interview in 1994 what made him want to write (*Face to Face* with Jeremy Isaacs, BBC2, 16 May), V. S. Naipaul had replied: 'An idea of nobility, a love of the smell of books, a love of the feel of books, a love of lettering, a wish to be famous – all these things'. The interview was given with a sense of ambitions having been fulfilled: Naipaul had twenty-four books to his name then, had been knighted recently (1990), had a bagful of literary awards (including the John Llewellyn Rhys Memorial Prize, the Hawthornden Prize, the Somerset Maugham Award, the Booker Prize, the Bennet Award, the T. S. Eliot Award, the Jerusalem Prize and the Trinity Cross from Trinidad), and had seen the opening of the Naipaul Archives at the University of Tulsa in 1994. It is interesting that at that moment of retrospection after having 'arrived' (his 1987 novel was entitled *The Enigma of Arrival*), the above-quoted sentiments express a youthful veneration for books, not simply as a medium for expression and creativity, but as tangible, sensual things. Naipaul's perspective of literature, and his contribution to it, is permeated with this sense of the tangibility of books. It is the basis of a peculiar sort of self-consciousness in his writing which is distinct from, and yet implicitly related to, the more overt levels of self-consciousness that are manifest therein.

Critical studies of Naipaul have frequently explored the other levels of self-consciousness that are manifest. All his books present an apprehension of his place in the world and an assessment of the world he inhabits (and Naipaul finds himself in a markedly cosmopolitan world) through excavations in time and place. His earlier books take him back in time: receding from his memories through the labyrinthine paths of family history to the hazy vista of Caribbean history itself. Starting from himself and his childhood Trinidad of the thirties and forties, he gradually draws his roots through the instabilities of an Indian Trinidadian family history of migrations and cultural adjustments, to the blurred colonial history of the Caribbean with its cryptic records, uncertain cultural definitions and redefinitions, shifting and disappearing populations. Even as this process unfolds, with the development of his *œuvre* Naipaul extends his gaze to other cultures. England forms a natural reference point because of her impact on the colonial society and past of his homeland; and as the country for which he left his homeland at the age of 18, where he began writing and eventually established himself, and where he ultimately settled down. India presents another obvious reference point for a Trinidadian Indian – Naipaul has written three substantial books and several articles about India. Besides, in the guise of a travel writer, Naipaul has also taken his preoccupations to other West Indian and South American countries, Iran, Indonesia, Malaysia, Pakistan, certain African countries, and the United States.

But in the midst of Naipaul's investigation and exposition of these themes and preoccupations, there is that self-awareness of being a writer of books – with his peculiar sense of their sensuality and tangibility, their complete and closed *thingness*. Arguably, this self-awareness guides the manner in which narratorial perspectives are arraigned, in which the forms are conceived, in which ultimately the social and political issues are presented. It is a self-consciousness which seeps beyond the committing of words to paper and enters the imaginative existence of his main protagonists. Characters in his books reflect the veneration for books which impinge upon their composition. It is in many ways a deep and true self-consciousness. But, I feel, it is also one that detracts from Naipaul's ostensible search for cultural 'truth' – which Naipaul has repeatedly used as his defence against detractors, and championed against his rivals (most recently in an interview in India where he asserted that 'magical realism', associated with Gabriel García Márquez, Günter Grass, and Salman Rushdie, takes writers away from the truth[1]). On the whole, Naipaul's books often reveal that which he is most anxious to avoid himself and expose in others: a certain superficiality of perception, a penchant for writing *books* as an end in itself,

2

rather than *writing* books as a means of communication. His books frequently present cultural judgements with an air of finality which his investigations do not warrant. I hope this is clarified and demonstrated to some extent below.

What follows is a brief critical survey of Naipaul's published books. It is informed by the above observations but does not focus exclusively on them. It is also informed by a general perspective of West Indian and other histories and literatures, by relatively recent studies of colonial and post-colonial discourses, by different sorts of ideologies and aesthetics, but doesn't lay a particular emphasis on any of these. Nor does the following attempt to dig further where Naipaul has dug already – assess the impact of his father Seepersad Naipaul's writings on him, for instance; or, for that matter, dig where Naipaul has not systematically delved himself – derive his development from his unpublished early-fifties stories,[2] or check his sources, for example. All these have been ably done by critics already: a select bibliography is in the usual location. What follows is a brief critical survey of Naipaul's published books. It should also be noted here that in a series entitled 'Writers and their Work' an active link between author and text is inevitably presumed; whatever the theoretical objections to such a presumption might be, what follows does try to establish a link between author and text.

3

2

The First Four Books

Naipaul has written often about the moment when he set out to write his first published book, *Miguel Street* (first written, but third to be published, in 1959). In Naipaul's world it is an almost epiphanic moment, when in 1954 'in a BBC room in London, on an old BBC typewriter, and on smooth, "non-rustle" BBC script paper, I wrote the first sentence of my first publishable book' ("Prologue to an Autobiography", FC 17). In 'Prologue to an Autobiography' he goes on to follow up the actual model for the first-mentioned character, Bogart, almost twenty years later (1977) in Venezuela. Naipaul was by then an established writer; he had found his vocation, and had, in a clear and material fashion, become embodied in his books. He describes the meeting of the personified author with the personified character: the meeting confirms the author's (almost prophetic) reading of the character in his book. And the description is predictably of a meeting which culminates in the concreteness of a book. The last sentences of the 'Prologue' read: 'In my eleventh month in London I wrote about Bogart. I wrote my book; I wrote another. I began to go back.' (FC 85). 'Going back', of course, also means 'going forward' for Naipaul.

In *Miguel Street* then one has the sanctioned beginning of the process of Naipaul's embodiment in books. It is a loosely connected collection of stories, each focused on a specific character who lives in a deprived neighbourhood in Port of Spain. Their separate aspirations and disappointments are fleetingly but carefully revealed. Apart from Bogart, the mysterious and taciturn bigamist who disappears from time to time, one encounters characters like Popo, the carpenter who doesn't build anything and is beset by marital discord; Elias, a

4

serious student who aspires to be a doctor but fails to pass most examinations; Man-Man, the mad man who unsuccessfully tries to re-enact Christ's crucifixion; B. Wordsworth (B for Black), the poet who believes he shares the heart of White Wordsworth, and never manages to sell any of his poems; Big Foot, 'really big and really black' and therefore intimidating, but actually a coward; Titus Hoyt, the teacher, who wrote letters to the newspaper on behalf of his students attesting to his own excellence; Mrs Hereira, whose affection for her lover is only answered by his brutality; Uncle Bhakcu, 'very nearly a mechanical genius' with a talent for destroying the most sturdy vehicles; Edward, who simply wanted to be American; Hat, in many ways the heart and soul of Miguel Street, who ends up in prison; and so on.

Even in that sparse list of characters some sense of the patterns which loosely link these fragments together begins to emerge. These are characters who are out of touch with the realities of their place and time, and of themselves. They invariably construct themselves and their ambitions in ways which are somehow impossible in Miguel Street: they are, so to say, 'out of joint' with their context, and are, in different ways, doomed. Their ambitions are usually framed in terms which are simply not rooted in Port of Spain: like B. Wordsworth's wanting to be a Wordsworthian poet (an interesting reiteration of the black writer who works with white models reappears in the shape of H. J. B. White in *Flag on the Island*, 1967), Edward's wanting to be American, and so on. The characters are not responsible: these stories are not of personal failure but of entrapment in a condition of cultural vacuum. The cultural vacuum is so complete that even the desire to be a doctor, or a mechanic, or a teacher – or in love – seems meaningless. As the stories unravel they appear to be a straightforward human-itarian celebration of a particular class of deprived and downtrodden people in Port of Spain; the implicit cultural critique becomes evident only in retrospect.

The retrospective view of the stories (it is significant, it is a *book* with all the sense of closure that is implied in that word) is underlined in the last section of *Miguel Street*. The first-person narratorial voice for all the stories is that of a boy (from child to adolescent) who lives on Miguel Street with his mother – unlike the young Naipaul in actual life, who lived in a large family. The ostensible narrator reports the events with all the enthusiasm and naive involvement of a child who lives among the characters he talks about and shares their aspirations and environment. The boy provides an inside perspective which, for the most part, does not allow the reader to draw the kind of links between stories drawn above, or the cultural critique to get clearly stated. In the last story, however, the insider perspective turns on itself; suddenly the boy enunciates his own view of things, and at that moment Trinidad is damned:

> 'You getting too wild,' my mother said.
> I paid her no attention until the time I drank so much in one evening that I remained drunk for two whole days afterwards. When I sobered up, I made a vow neither to smoke nor drink again.
> I said to my mother, 'Is not my fault really. Is just Trinidad. What else anyone can do here except drink?' (*MS* 167)

Soon after that the boy is easily tempted by Ganesh Pundit (of whom more soon) to go to England, inappropriately as a student in 'drugs', with a scholarship:

> Ganesh said, 'Think. It mean going to London. It mean seeing snow and seeing the Thames and seeing the big Parliament.'
> I said, 'All right. I go study drugs.' (*MS* 168)

That view of cultural displacement is all that takes the boy away in the last lines of the book, and as the *real* narrator, who now appears clearly, declares there, he was 'destined to be gone for good' (*MS* 171). At this point the full extent of retrospection in *Miguel Street*, and its function as cultural critique, is conveyed. The boy-narrator is simply a narratorial device, the real narrator speaks from beyond the end of the book, and returns his readers to the past tense of the first sentence of the book: 'Every morning when he got up Hat would sit on the banister of his back verandah and shout across, "What happening there, Bogart?"' (*MS* 9). *Miguel Street* is a considered and closed cultural judgement which emerges from the retrospection of the invisible real narrator and lies in the future for the ostensible boy-narrator.

Miguel Street dexterously combines a cultural critique, a sense of the closure of the book, and certain interesting distantiating techniques. This combination is repeated with different

6

emphases and foci, and increasing degrees of self-consciousness and cohesiveness, in the following three books.

If *Miguel Street* is a collection of stories about failure, the next two books, and the first two to be published, *The Mystic Masseur* (1957) and *The Suffrage of Elvira* (1958), are, in a manner of speaking, success stories. The mystic masseur is Pundit Ganesh Ramsumair of Fuente Grove, who, with the help of an uncomfortable and mediocre education and an unremunerative marriage, starts off as a teacher, tries to become a masseur in the family tradition, and becomes a recognized psychic and healer instead. He is thereafter accepted as a representative of the Hindu community in Trinidad, expands his sphere of influence by using and eventually writing books, establishes himself discreetly and pre-eminently successfully as an entrepreneur, joins politics and succeeds in getting elected as a Member of the Legislative Council, is eventually distinguished by an MBE, and ultimately makes an appearance in London as a Colonial Statesman who passes under the name of G. Ramsay Muir. In *The Suffrage of Elvira*, Surujpat Harbans, who owns a transport company, makes a bid for election to the Legislative Council from Elvira, and eventually wins. The book describes the process in detail: it involves placating Baksh by taking on his son as campaign manager (Baksh controls the Muslim votes), wooing Chittaranjan by promising to marry his daughter to Harbans's son (Chittaranjan controls the Hindu votes), countering Preacher's rival bid on the strength of support within the black community, and neutralizing the threats posed by a couple of Jehovah's Witnesses and a mongrel which becomes the object of superstitious fear. Put together, the two books could be read as Naipaul's view of society and politics in forties and early fifties Trinidad – both examine personages who reach the upper echelons of the colonial establishment in Trinidad. Pundit Ganesh is elected as MLA in 1946 and nominated as such in 1950, and the elections described in *The Suffrage of Elvira* occur in 1950.

It might be useful at this stage to have a concise description of the political context which Naipaul addresses. The period between 1910 and 1936 saw a rapid growth in political consciousness in Trinidad (and the West Indies generally) and in the desire for self-determination. Several factors contributed

to this. Trinidadian Indian organizations to represent Indian
interests had existed since the late nineteenth century, notably
the East Indian National Association and the East Indian
National Congress (formed in 1909, primarily middle-class).
The growth of an industrial sector centred on oil-field workers
(predominantly Afro-Caribbean) since 1910, gave rise eventually
to Trade Union organizations and a left movement (albeit
deeply divided). For the black population extraneous political
influences were also a significant factor: the Harlem Renaissance
(in which the West Indian poet Claude McKay was an important
figure), Marcus Garvey's Back-to-Africa movement, W. E. B.
Dubois's and Booker T. Washington's incisive analyses of the
condition of black people in America. Anti-colonial hackles were
raised at the indifference with which western powers treated
Mussolini's annexation of Abyssinia in 1936. After 1924 seven of
the twenty-six-member Legislative Council in Trinidad were
designated to be elected by an electorate of six per cent of the
population. The worsening economic crisis in the Depression
years of the thirties led to unrest, culminating in the oilworkers'
strike in 1937, organized largely under the leadership of Uriah
Butler. The predominantly Indian Trinidad Sugar Estates and
Factory Workers Union also joined the strike. Working-class
unrest and militant nationalism eventually led to the British
government deciding to concede elected representation in
Trinidad and Tobago, though it was postponed till after the
second world war. With the support of a sympathetic post-war
Labour government in Britain elections with universal adult
suffrage were held in Trinidad in 1946. Only half the seats in the
Legislative Council were put up for election, the rest being
reserved for members nominated by the Governor or for senior
civil servants. The same system was followed in 1950. Both the
1946 and the 1950 elections were marked by the failure of the
radical and left-oriented organizations to consolidate their
position (largely due to internal divisions), the success of the
Indian middle class, and the debilitating influx of the race factor
in electoral politics. Ranjit Kumar, president of the East India
National Congress, for instance, contested elections from the
County of Victoria in 1946 and won by playing the race card. He
thereafter wrote a 'minority report' arguing that a largely black
majority party wouldn't be able to deal fairly with the Indian

population, and called for communal representation. On the other hand, a more integrationist political formation was also beginning to emerge. After the 1950 elections the single largest group in the Legislative Council was the Butler Party. Uriah Butler (who had lost the 1946 elections) decided to present an oil–sugar front in 1950 – of the six seats that the Butler Party won, four were represented by Indians. Indians had also throughout been associated with the left-leaning and trade union organizations. The trade union leader Adrian Cola Rienzi was an Indian originally named Krishna Deonarine. However, after 1952, racial party politicking was aggravated with the formation of the Hindu organization the Sanatan Dharma Mahasabha, and the political party People's Democratic Party (PDP), under the leadership of B. S. Maraj. It was challenged by Dr Eric Williams's People's National Movement (PNM). In the 1956 elections the first single-party government was formed by the PNM, which won again in 1961, and saw Trinidad through independence in 1962.

The point of this skeletal description of the political context is that it is, despite the deep communal and racial divisions and ideological polarities, far from being vapid or passive: in it ideas, ideologies and demagogues are active, and recently subjugated peoples (from several margins and minorities) are demonstrably in the process of becoming determinative political agents rather than submissive functionaries. The point of the context is also that it doesn't appear with any clarity in either of the two novels in question. The successes of *The Mystic Masseur* and *The Suffrage of Elvira* are of course meant to be, and are convincingly portrayed as, profound failures. Ganesh Pundit's career generally, and especially his political career, is a continuous series of accommodations to predetermined social attitudes and expectations. He deftly falls into roles which are allocated to him in a caste-, religious community-, race-, and class-riven society; he is driven by a sense of fulfilling a preordained role (as he maintains often in his books); he presents images, and chameleon-like changes images subtly, according to require-ments. It is made clear that there is no Ganesh point of view, there are simply an assortment of images which Ganesh creates because he is expected to. His career moves predictably towards the ultimate accommodation of becoming a champion of colonial rule in Trinidad, and finally losing his identity to the fake 'G. Ramsay Muir, MBE.'

The description of electoral politics in *The Suffrage of Elvira* is also that of a political ethos which is entirely devoid of any ideological involvement or commitment, where political strategies are determined by the given structures of society and the narrowest self-interests. The three communal groups (Christians, Hindus, Muslims) and the two racial groups (black and coloured) are unchangeably fixed in their given communal and racial alignments; not even the idea of rising above these or changing these can be mooted. The only other factors which can impinge upon this society are irrational ones, like the *obeah*[1] mongrel or the Jehovah's witnesses. The aberrations – like the Muslim Baksh's son being the Hindu Harbans's campaign manager, or the Hindu Lorkhoor canvassing on the black Christian Preacher's behalf – can only be explained in terms of self-interest. The only operative modes of communication in the books are ultimately financial.

The impression that the two novels convey is similar to the one obtained in *Miguel Street*: that of a society of passive individuals who might have individual ambition and promise but are incapable of fulfilling them or of effecting any larger social change. On the whole, it is the picture of a passive people in a stultified society. Passivity pervades the greater picture discernible in the three books examined so far, and determines the presentation of detail. For instance, consider Naipaul's use of calypso[2] in *Miguel Street* and in *The Mystic Masseur* – the calypso about which he was to write the following in *The Middle Passage* in 1962:

> It is only in calypso that the Trinidadian touches reality. The calypso is a purely local form. No form composed outside Trinidad is a calypso. The calypso deals with local incidents, local attitudes, and does so in a local language. The pure calypso, the best calypso, is incomprehensible to the outsider. (*MP* 75–6)

For Naipaul, calypso is a record of events and their effects in Trinidad from a purely Trinidadian point of view. It is in that sense that all the calypso lyrics cited in *Miguel Street* and *The Mystic Masseur* are used. They come at the end of stories, like references from an oral text which wittily condense the events in the stories; to Naipaul calypso provides a folk archive. What Naipaul's presentation of the calypso seems consistently to overlook is that it isn't simply a passive record or archive, it is also an affective medium. By its very nature the most renowned calypsonians – such as the Mighty Sparrow, whom Naipaul quotes – were as much performers as lyric and song writers. And any survey of the history of calypso[3] demonstrates that from its inception in slave songs (often subversive protest songs, ridiculing employers), and especially in its use in the thirties (when legislation was brought in to ensure that calypsonians were required to submit their compositions for police scrutiny prior to public performance) and forties (when Albert Gomes used the calypso as a medium for political campaigning), the calypso has as often been a mode of political intervention and subversion as of commentary and reflection of local attitudes.

Naipaul's use of the calypso evokes only a small part of what calypso consists of. Naipaul's presentation of the social and political picture is only a partial picture, though it is made to seem all-subsuming and complete. But why does this happen in Naipaul's presentation of Trinidad? It is not sufficient to argue that Naipaul is limited by his focus on Indian Trinidadians – though largely conservative and sectarian in the 1946 and 1950 elections, there were also amongst them progressive elements. Even the conservative and sectarian elements were not simply passive shadows of their allocated roles, they were active reactionary agents often motivated beyond self-interest. Besides, Naipaul's novels do, despite the Indian Trinidadian foreground, actually extend their observations to other communities, especially the black community, and fix them in the same passivity, and in images of well-worn racial stereotypes. I do not dwell on Naipaul's racism here: it appears in many of his writings and is discussed later. Nor is the assertion that Naipaul's perspective of Trinidad politics and society is simply moulded by his own Hindu upbringing and mentality wholly satisfactory. It seems to me that Naipaul deliberately and self-consciously discourages that approach. The narratorial perspectives in *The Mystic Masseur* and *The Suffrage of Elvira* are designed to undercut any hypothesis of a Naipaul perspective. Even the device of the boy-narrator, used so effectively in *Miguel Street*, is withdrawn in a self-

11

conscious fashion. He makes a cameo appearance at the beginning of *The Mystic Masseur* and then more or less disappears. Instead there appears an omniscient narrator, speaking in a faintly amused and quite remote voice, observing without commitment. The ironical inflection and noncommittal amusement in this voice is not consistent with the exposition of a philosophically or psychologically coloured view of society. It is as effective a distanciation technique in the context of this sort of social and political overview, as the boy-narrator had been a familiarizing technique in the presentation of deprived households in Miguel Street. It gives the social and political picture, with its sense of meaninglessness and narrowness and meanness and sheer passivity, a peculiar air of detachment and authenticity.

But it is neither detached nor authentic. It is no more than a particular limited representation of a context. If it comes across as both it is because it is stylistically designed to do so: it proffers, to revive a point made above, its air of completion and closure as a book. Despite the dates and a few vestiges of references to a real history, both novels create enclosed and coherent worlds which do not depend in any way on extraneous reference. The rationale of what happens in them is begun and completed within their pages. *The Mystic Masseur* suggests, for instance, that Pundit Ganesh's career and experiences are something central to the experience of all Trinidad (though Ganesh's sphere is actually a small part of Trinidad), and that something significant about the condition of Trinidad and its peoples in general has been conveyed (rather than just about the Hindu Trinidad of the forties). Similarly Elvira, in *The Suffrage of Elvira*, which appears to be curiously insulated from the rest of Trinidad, is made out to be a microcosmic representation of the macrocosm. Though these novels ostensibly refer to a specific period in history, they are presented with a sense of closure (of self-containment) which renders their observations more general. Critics feel tempted to observe (too many have done so to be referred to here) that it is irrelevant to look at the actual Trinidadian history of the forties to assess these novels. Naipaul, they argue, has created a world which should not be perceived in historical terms, but rather in terms of broader and deeper insights into a certain culture and society; it is the general life in the specific history that he evokes. Texts, in other words, especially Naipaul's books, should be understood in their own true-to-life terms rather than in terms of historical records: and yet, in view of the historical events mentioned above, Naipaul's cultural evaluation cannot but be regarded as problematic.

No one is more aware than Naipaul in these two novels of the dubiousness of the 'reality' of books, and – to take the awareness of books to a level remarked before – the sensuality and tangibility of books. This awareness is presented through the main protagonists in both novels. Ganesh Pundit in *The Mystic Masseur* obsessively collects books with little regard for their content:

> 'Leela,' Ganesh said, 'The boy want to know how much book it have here.'
> 'Let me see,' Leela said, and hitched up the broom to her waistband. She started to count off the fingers of her left hand. 'Four hundred Everyman, two hundred Penguin – six hundred. Six hundred, and one hundred Reader's Library, make seven hundred. I think with all the other book it have about fifteen hundred good book here.'
> The taxi driver whistled, and Ganesh smiled. (*MM* 15)

Ganesh's disciples are impressed by the fact that he has those books rather than by his having read them; Ganesh takes a large number of books to his public addresses, more for the impact of their presence than their usefulness; and Ganesh sets out to be a writer for the sake of writing a book rather than because he has something to write about (not unlike Naipaul, judging from the Jeremy Isaacs interview). In *The Suffrage of Elvira* the efficacy of texts is not presented in terms of books but in terms of election slogans. The emphasis on the visibility and tangibility of the slogan is not, however, dissimilar to Ganesh's demonstrative 'use' of books. The election campaign at Elvira is to a large degree a war of words: between Foam (Baksh's son and Harbans's campaign manager), who has a facility with words and slogans, and Lorkhoor (Preacher's campaigner), who also has a way with words and eventually finds his *métier* in journalism. The moment of foreboding and confusion is announced when the slogan 'Vote Harbans or Die' becomes mysteriously 'Die, Die, Die', and Harbans's victory becomes certain when Foam manages to neutralize the 'Die, Die, Die' slogan by associating it with the ripped up *obeah* dog and incriminating the Jehovah's Witnesses. Words and books convey a truth not so much because they say truthful things but because they *are* indelibly there.

It is this preoccupation with the tangibility and indelibility of words, of texts, of books, that lead more squarely to *A House for Mr Biswas* (1961), Naipaul's fourth and most successful book. *A House for Mr Biswas* is an imaginative reconstruction of Naipaul's father Seepersad Naipaul's (1906–53) life. Seepersad Naipaul, like Mr Biswas, came from a rural Hindu background, had somehow established himself as a journalist for the *Trinidad Guardian* (for which he had written sensationalistic and colourful articles), and aspired to be a writer of stories. Some of his stories were collected and published as *Gurudeva and Other Indian Tales* in 1943. Of these stories Naipaul was to write in his 'Prologue to an Autobiography':

> These stories celebrated Indian village life, and the Hindu rituals that gave grace and completeness to that life. They also celebrated elemental things, the order of the working day, the labour of the rice-fields, the lighting of the cooking fire in the half-walled gallery of a thatched hut, the preparation and eating of food. (FC 42)

Seeparsad Naipaul also shared Mr Biswas's dissatisfaction with the Hindu community which defined him, and his scepticism towards conservative Hinduism and its communal rituals and conventions. Though Naipaul wasn't aware of it at the time of writing *A House for Mr Biswas*, Seeparsad Naipaul was victimized for criticizing animal sacrifices in Hindu rituals and consequently had a nervous breakdown – Naipaul has mentioned this often in later interviews and writings.[4] Naipaul evidently came to regard the twelve years he had spent with his father, and the ideas about writing and reading which he shared with his father, as a sort of apprenticeship.

There are two strands in *A House for Mr Biswas*: one describes the various domestic environments which Mr Biswas had inhabited from childhood onwards, his experiences in these, and final escape from these into his own house; the other strand delineates Mr Biswas's growth from being a sign-painter to becoming a journalist and, in his own wishful way, a man of letters and lover of books. The first strand takes off from his early childhood in the house of his father and mother, Raghu and Bipti; moves into the prosperous environs of his aunt Tara's and her husband Ajodha's establishment, and from there to brief sojourns in the houses of several of the latter's dependants; then, by marriage to Shama, his move to the Tusli household in Hanuman House. Mr Biswas's association with the Tulsi household, an extended family governed by Mrs Tulsi and her son-in-law Seth, occupies the larger part of the book; in it Mr Biswas gradually develops as the family rebel with a strong desire to find his own separate space. Escape bids take Mr Biswas to the Chase as an aspiring shopkeeper, to Green Vale as a sub-overseer, to Port of Spain as a reasonably successful journalist, and he even has a brief spell in government service. But he fails to disembroil his own and his family's life from the Tulsi household, and continues to find himself relocated in different Tulsi establishments – Hanuman House, the Tulsi house at Port of Spain, the Shorthills House. He finally makes his escape when he buys a rather ramshackle house on Sikkim Street in Port of Spain, where he settles down with his family, from where his son Anand (based on Naipaul himself) leaves for England, and where he eventually dies.

Interwoven with the ups and downs of Mr Biswas's search for domestic independence is the second strand: Mr Biswas's growth as a writer and lover of books. This is linked to his first successful career as a sign-painter, which is also his first apprehension of the tangibility of words and of the possibility of escape into an alternative reality of words:

> his hand became surer, his strokes bolder, his feelings for letters finer. He thought R and S the most beautiful Roman letters; no letter could express so many moods as R, without losing its beauty; and what could compare with the swing and rhythm of S? With a brush, large letters were easier than small, and he felt much satisfaction after he and Alec had covered long stretches of paling with signs for Pluko, which was good for the hair in various ways, and Anchor cigarettes. (*HB* 76)

This career is abandoned in the claustrophobic environment of the Tulsi household, only to be resumed again as soon as he really manages to escape from the Tulsis to Port of Spain. In the interim Mr Biswas hones his sensitivity to words by using them against sundry members of the Tulsi family whom he dislikes and studying newspaper cuttings. His revisiting of the sign-painter's profession leads him almost directly into the offices of the *Sentinel* and an apprenticeship in the journalistic career, where he starts off by trying to impress the editor with his eclectic reading. What he learns at the *Sentinel* office is not so much the art of faithful reportage as the art of embellishing stories in words, transforming mundane events into eye-catching, sensational, and fantastic stories. In the act of creating the journalistic text Mr Biswas acquires the ability to comprehend and yet evade reality; the journalistic story becomes the site of contending realities, one following the rationale of daily existence and happenings and the other following the rationale of a good catchy story. This mode of escape into the alternative reality of the story, and the lure of producing a book (a result of his inborn reverence for books as such irrespective of their relevance to him) soon turns into a desire to translate his own life into a story. Predictably, his first attempt at story-writing begins with his own experiences and is tellingly entitled 'Escape' (*HB* 345). In the latter part of *A House for Mr Biswas* the hero gradually retreats, after brief flirtations with literary groups and schools and with growing dissatisfaction in his journalistic career, into a world of unfinished stories and scraps of eccentrically gleaned information and quotations from books. Mr Biswas only gives up this preoccupation when he finally achieves his own space and a fulfilment of sorts.

In the latter part of the book other characters also enter the magic of words in the bid to escape. The frenetic examination preparations for the children is described with verve – academic achievement was the only escape from the constraints of Hindu Trinidad (exemplified in Naipaul's own life). And yet there is a farcical dissociation between learning or knowledge and the tangibility of the written word or books:

> He was the eldest Tuttle boy. He had impressed his parents by a constant demand for exercise books and by a continuous show of writing. He said he was making notes. In fact he had copied out every word of *Nelson's West Indian Geography*, by Captain Cutteridge, Director of Education, author of *Nelson's West Indian Readers* and *Nelson's West Indian Arithmetics*. He had completed the *Geography* in more than a dozen exercise books, and was at the moment engaged on the first volume of *Nelson's West Indian History*, by Captain Daniel, Assistant Director of Education. (*HB* 463)

But, unlike *Miguel Street*, escape from Trinidad as actual departure is counterpoised against Mr Biswas's own special mode of escape into the tangibility and alternative reality of the text itself, of books. Somehow the actual departures – Owad's and Anand's – seem to lead to far less satisfactory escapes than Mr Biswas's own into words.

Several levels of self-consciously welded preoccupations are manifest in Naipaul's first four works of fiction. The heart of these, it is suggested above, is a self-consciousness of the tangibility and sensuality, of the self-containedness and reality, of the closure and indelibility of books. This provides the imperative behind Naipaul's reading and writing, and this is what Naipaul self-consciously achieves and what his readers unavoidably receive of Naipaul. It operates behind the scenes in the manner in which his fiction is conceived and in the deployment of narratorial techniques. It is brought into focus by being displayed within the fiction, as a theme which occupies some of the characters. More overtly, the early fiction addresses the state of Trinidadian culture, politics, and society. This involves an intelligently presented partial representation of the Trinidad of the thirties and the forties. The point underlying this partial presentation, which is made to appear comprehensive, is the paucity of that society, its narrowness, passivity, con-servatism, incohesiveness, and lack of authenticity. Lack of authenticity in brief is what Naipaul finds in Trinidad: individuals who entertain aspirations which make little sense in Trinidad, a culture which treasures texts and ideas which are patently out of place, a politics which follows imperatives which contradict its purpose, and which lack any ideological commit-ment. These books might have been the most vituperative Juvenalian satire if Naipaul didn't sieve them through carefully constructed narratorial perspectives to mellow the effect, like the ostensible boy-narrator of *Miguel Street*, and the remote, amused (full of 'jokes', or 'jokey', as Naipaul prefers to call it), noncommittal, omniscient narrator which is found in the other books. 'Is the cultural pessimism deserved?' one feels obliged to ask. There are two possible answers: (a) yes, because it is the truth; (b) no, because Naipaul has perversely misrepresented Trinidad. Justifications can be found for both answers (though the case for the latter seems to me to be stronger); more importantly, both answers throw up further questions. If this is the truth about Trinidad, how can it be explained? There are implicit indicators in the books: one needs to look into the history of Trinidad's colonial past, and the histories of discrete communities within that, to grasp the paucity of Trinidadian society as Naipaul depicts it. This doesn't happen in a lucid fashion in the early fiction, but Naipaul returns to the issue later.

Further questions crop up. If Trinidad presents for Naipaul an unsatisfactory culture, what is a satisfactory culture for him? What are his criteria for judging the authenticity of a culture and society? Is it possible that Naipaul's cultural values actually lead him to present a distorted view of Trinidad, rather than a truthful one? In his following books Naipaul delves further to answer these questions, both by going back in history, and by providing comparative cultural critiques. Arguably, in doing this Naipaul doesn't simply clarify his thinking in his own terms – his thinking gets *revealed* in ways which he might not have intended or expected.

3

More Fiction

A House for Mr Biswas was published in 1961. In the sixties V. S. Naipaul produced non-fictional books in which the insularity of the Trinidad, especially the Hindu Trinidad, described in his first four books gives way to an apprehension of Trinidad within broader cultural and historical horizons. This endeavour was set in motion by a fellowship from the government of Trinidad and Tobago to write a book on the Caribbean, which resulted in *The Middle Passage* (1962) – a sweeping appraisal of cultural distinctions and similarities between, and cultural influences and interactions manifest in, Caribbean countries. The other end of the decade (1969) saw the appearance of *The Loss of El Dorado*, an eclectic rendering of the history of Trinidad (and the Caribbean generally). This reorientation of his perspective of Trinidad within a larger perspective of the Caribbean is examined later. My more immediate concern is with the fiction that Naipaul published in this decade (all of which benefited from this reoriented perspective): *Mr Stone and the Knights Companion* (1963), a novel set entirely in England; *The Mimic Men* (1967), a novel which shuttles back and forth between England and the Caribbean; and *A Flag on the Island* (1967), a collection of short stories written between 1954 and 1965 which moves from the Caribbean to England and back to the Caribbean with a visible change of attitude.

Naipaul was preparing himself for this reoriented perspective even while he was at work on *A House for Mr Biswas*. In 1958 he wrote an essay for the *Times Literary Supplement* in which he contemplated writing about England. In talking about the prejudice of the European towards the non-European writer he remarks there:

The only way out is to cease being a regional writer. People who wish me well have urged me to do so before it is too late. They say I have lived long enough in England to write about England. I would like nothing better. But there are difficulties.

The English writer benefits by travel but the foreign writer who comes to England benefits less. (*OB* 14)

He goes on to argue, perhaps facetiously, that the English writer abroad is usually in a position to observe other cultures because they are open (like the windows in the warm Caribbean), while the non-English writer visiting England is unlikely to have the same advantage since the English conduct their lives behind closed doors (to avoid draughts). Clearly this wasn't Naipaul's problem because he had found his way into English interiors: *Mr Stone and the Knights Companion* is the result. More interestingly, in the same article Naipaul also writes about the paradox of his situation at that stage: he observes that 'the social comedies I write can be fully appreciated only by someone who knows the region I write about. Without that knowledge it is easy for my books to be dismissed as farces and my characters as eccentrics'; and yet he admits that he 'write[s] for England' (*OB* 11) and depends on an English readership.

In other words, Naipaul contemplates a reoriented perspective because he realizes the schismatic position he holds as a writer and feels a desire to overcome it, to establish a more harmonious relationship between his books, his readers, and himself. In a sense Naipaul had expressed a schismatic self-awareness earlier. In the previous chapter I discussed the dual preoccupation of Naipaul's early fiction: a consciousness of the tangibility and reality of books, and a preoccupation with the social and political ethos of Trinidad. There is, I have argued, a paradoxical relationship between the two: the former allows the latter to be presented as possessed of an air of passivity, of being meaningless, of being a sham, of being claustrophobic; while books can provide an escape from that sham and a commitment to an indelible reality – books evoke, by their very tangibility, authority and truth. And yet texts and books themselves throw up an endless potential for distortion and manipulation and deception, just as Naipaul's characters use books and texts in manipulative ways, and Naipaul can arguably be seen to distort history and present it selectively. This paradox is analogous to the paradox of his position as a Trinidadian writer who writes for an English readership: schisms run across both levels of self-awareness. It is this schismatic self-awareness which begins to get clarified as he reconsiders his perspective of Trinidad, and the Caribbean generally – it offers a potential relief from his problematic position as a writer of books about the Caribbean for the English.

The schismatic self-awareness finds a somewhat different sort of clarification in another short article, entitled 'Jasmine', published in the *Times Literary Supplement* in 1964. In this Naipaul argues that there is an inevitable displacement involved in the attitude to English language and literature that a Trinidadian can entertain. Trinidad is (with different inflections) primarily English-speaking, but the literature that is associated with and implicit in the English language, and which is (or rather, *was* in the forties and fifties) therefore almost exclusively read and studied in Trinidad, is alien to that culture. Books of English literature are fantastic and unreal in the Trinidadian context, and yet they acquire a deceptive sense of reality which cannot be overcome unless the Trinidadian is exposed to England, as Naipaul was. The irony is, as Naipaul neatly puts it, that to the Trinidadian the jasmine flower, which is easily found in the Caribbean, seems exotic, while the daffodil (of Wordsworthian fame), which doesn't grow in the Caribbean, seems familiar.

The reorientation of perspective, the bid to rise above regionalism, the move towards finding coherence in a paradoxical position – all these are located to a large extent in Naipaul's least considered novel, *Mr Stone and the Knights Companion*. Usually regarded as an oddity amongst Naipaul's books, it is remembered primarily as an attempt at a quintessentially *English* novel which is set entirely in England and presents exclusively English characters. This novel is largely about removal and alienation. The main protagonists of the novel are all in different ways, and often desperately, lonely. Their loneliness is charted through, though not alleviated by, the routines to which they habitually adhere. The 62-year-old Mr Stone's establishment, his ritualistic bachelor existence, his awkwardness in social gatherings, his undemanding and unimaginative office life, his hallucinatory moments in the underground station, are described in some detail to convey this loneliness. Mrs Springer's advent into this existence, through marriage, is itself motivated by her loneliness, and the relationship constantly struggles against it. A brief entry into Whymper's life – and Whymper, despite the name, seems to exude confidence – also reveals a life bereft of companionship and dominated by sexual fantasies. The great project at the heart of the book, around which the lives of these characters gradually begin to revolve, has to do with loneliness too: the Knights Companion is Mr Stone's brainchild, fleshed out by Whymper, and is meant to provide companionship and a social outlet for pensioners. The setting up of the Knights Companion affords a fleeting insight into other lonely lives in different parts of England. The generalization of the condition, and the descriptions of rituals and social conventions which seem designed to accommodate it, suggests that alienation is the core of this book not because Naipaul chooses to focus on a peculiarly socially inept group of characters but because it is an unavoidable aspect of English culture.

It is alienation almost as a cultural phenomenon that *Mr Stone and the Knights Companion* presents. It is not, I feel convinced, an existentialist condition which unifies all humanity irrespective of their contexts – whether in the colonial margin (Trinidad) or the colonizing centre (England) – as some critics have suggested.[1] Mr Biswas's alienation is of a quite different nature from Mr Stone's, and the difference is conditional to their discrete contexts. Mr. Stone's alienation places him in England, Mr Biswas's makes him impotently long for escape; Mr Stone is one of many, Mr Biswas is one against many; Mr Stone's alienation makes him ordinary (he becomes extraordinary when he rises above it briefly), Mr Biswas's makes him strange (he becomes ordinary when he stifles his out-of-jointness).

The manifestation of Englishness in a kind of cultural alienation is what the novel presents, and its cultural remoteness is emphasized. There are fleeting apprehensions of this distance, of the insularity of England and the English. Gwen's trying to do Shylock in a Jewish accent, or Margaret's pretending that in India people roast pieces of cake on skewers over fires, are moments of absurd and grotesque connection with non-English cultures which creep into the world of the novel. The best subtext to the novel as a whole, to its deliberate delving into an English interior so remote and tranquil as to be inconsequential, probably appears in the following quotation:

> The entrance to the Underground station was filthy; in a street across the road a meeting of the British National Party was in progress, a man shouting himself hoarse from the back of a van. Behind neon lights and steaming glass windows the new-style coffee houses were packed; and the streets were full of young people in art-student dress and foreigners of every colour.
>
> The address Mrs Springer gave turned out to be a private hotel in one of the crescents off Earl's Court Road. A small typewritten 'Europeans Only' card below the bell proclaimed it a refuge of respectability and calm. (*SKC* 26)

Except for that brief flash of colour – foreigners and art students – one might have forgotten that this is the late fifties and early sixties: the period of exultant decolonizations around the world (including Trinidad), the period of angry young men in English writing, of counter-cultural expressions, of civil rights protests, on the eve of a new left movement: the sixties scarcely need to be rehearsed. But this is a fleeting evocation of the time; the novel retreats from there into a 'Europeans Only' zone, so removed and exclusive that fascist proclamations of national (and racial) exclusiveness, glimpsed in the British National Party meeting, seem (not unnatural) unnecessary. At the same moment a reader might be struck by the irony of this smooth retreat into the 'Europeans Only' refuge of 'respectability and calm', since it does ultimately issue from the pen of V. S. Naipaul – who is unlikely to have had access to any such English interior on those terms.

But apart from the characterization of remoteness and alienation in English culture, how does Naipaul's appraisal of that culture differ from cultural appraisals in his Trinidad novels? If the attitudes to cultural appraisal that are manifest in the early Trinidad novels and in this first England novel (so to say) are compared, one becomes aware of certain significant *negative* features of *Mr Stone and the Knights Companion*, not features which are thrown up by the latter, but features which the earlier novels had thrown up and which *are not* evidenced in the latter. To put it briefly, the Trinidad novels (and, much more explicitly, *The Middle Passage*) presented cultural critique – the Caribbean is marked by its intrinsic lack of direction and purposelessness, harbouring aspirations which do not make sense in its context (alienation in Trinidad is identified accordingly), a passivity which renders it peculiarly vulnerable to extrinsic determination, an absorption in selfish pecuniary interests, a penchant for mimicry (a term which Naipaul increasingly deploys in examinations of so-called Third World cultures) or for imitation of inappropriate English and American values and mores, and a claustrophobic environment which underlines the need for escape. These provide the criteria for cultural evaluation in his early fiction and (as examined below) non-fiction. There is no cultural critique in a comparable sense in *Mr Stone and the Knights Companion*. There is more of an air of documentation here. Englishness is alienated and remote and ignorant, but it is self-possessed; English characters do not look outwards, they withdraw into themselves; despite all alienation and remotenesss the English characters represent an active principle; along with the alienation and remoteness, there is a social conscience which rises above simple self-interest and leads to fulfilment of a sort. Mr Stone's and Whymper's Knights Companion scheme is an instance of such an active principle, which extends across an ingrained English alienation the possibility of contact, and to work for which neither Whymper nor Mr Stone are motivated merely by self-interest (these interests get served anyway). That dissatisfactions remain is not so much an indication of failure as a promise of new directions – the success of what Mr Stone started is taken over by the younger Whymper. And even for Mr Stone the final note that is struck in the novel is not one of despair or the need to escape, but one of repose:

> He was no destroyer. Once before the world had collapsed around him. But he had survived. And he had no doubt that in time calm would come to him again. Now he was only very tired. (*SKC* 126)

This absence of cultural critique and the generally (despite incidental disparagement) more affirmative note in the appraisal of England presented in the novel is most trenchantly conveyed in the attitude of the omniscient narrator who appears here. This is not the amused and somewhat patronizing narratorial voice – deliberately distanced from the context it speaks of, issuing from and addressed to a region beyond and outside the culture it delineates – that was consistently available in the early novels. The language (an educated standard

English) of this omniscient narrator is not immediately at odds with the native varieties of Trinidadian English the characters speak in Naipaul's early novels. It is a narratorial voice which is witty in a predictable and rather dull fashion, a kind of extension of the dull wit which Mr Stone himself appreciates – a narratorial voice, in short, which gives the impression of being much more reconciled and fitted to its function as such.

Possible answers to the questions that were raised at the end of the previous chapter (if Trinidad presents for Naipaul an unsatisfactory culture, what is a satisfactory culture for him?; what are his criteria for judging the authenticity of a culture and society?) come to mind. To say that a comparative analysis of the modes of cultural appraisal in the early fiction and in the English novel leads one to suspect that the latter represents (with a few reservations) the paradigm – a satisfactory, coherent, and authentic culture – might be simplistic. It might also be an over-reading of *Mr Stone and the Knights Companion*. But it is not far off the point, so long as one keeps Naipaul's obvious reservations about, and the expository (as opposed to evaluative) approach to, English culture in mind. The expository mode of writing about England ensures that Naipaul's opinions about England can only be inferred, they cannot be ascertained with reference to any specific statement. However, the suspicion that a perception of Englishness (or broadly First-Worldness) provides the frame of Naipaul's cultural critiques of Trinidad, the Caribbean, the Third World, can be strengthened by examining both the other books of fiction that appeared in the sixties: *A Flag on the Island* and *The Mimic Men*.

Both *A Flag on the Island* and *The Mimic Men* present, unlike any of the fiction he had written prior to that, bridges between the self-consciously differentiated First and Third Worlds (descriptive terms I use despite their obvious limitations). In *A Flag on the Island*, a collection of short stories, it is largely a matter of juxtaposition and of the experimental displacement of narratorial voices – especially in the title story which is placed last. *The Mimic Men* is the story of Ralph Singh, a person of Indian origin, whose ostensibly autobiographical narrative moves effortlessly between the Caribbean island of his birth and London – but between the effortless shifts there are subtle changes of perspective which give meaning to the title.

25

The stories in *A Flag on the Island* could be divided into three categories. In the first category could be placed those which seem to be extensions of his early fiction, which examine related themes and use by-now familiar narratorial ploys, and some of which were indeed written while the early fiction was being written. There are stories which deal with childhood experiences ('The Raffle', 1957; 'The Mourners', 1950); and those which deal with characters from the Trinidad of Naipaul's childhood ('My Aunt Gold Teeth', 1954; 'The Heart', 1960; and most interesting of these, 'The Enemy', 1955, which gives a somewhat different view of Naipaul's mother from her characterization as Shama in *A House for Mr Biswas*). The second category could include the two stories which, like *Mr Stone and the Knights Companion*, focus primarily on English characters in England ('Greenie and Yellow', 1957; 'The Perfect Tenants', 1957). The juxtaposition of these two categories mainly confirms the observations made above with regard to stylistic nuances and narratorial attitude in the early fiction and *Mr Stone and the Knights Companion*. However, the form of the short story, particularly Naipaul's use of the short story to present almost naturalistic vignettes of life, doesn't allow for any pointed cultural critique to be presented, discerned or compared. The third category, and in my view the most significant, should include the stories where Naipaul, for the first time in his published works, offers narratorial voices which emulate characters who are not omniscient or identifiable with the author. This occurs in 'A Christmas Story' (1962) apparently narrated by a self-righteous Trinidadian Indian Christian schoolteacher; more tentatively in 'The Night Watchman's Occurrence Book', (1962); in 'The Baker's Story' (1962), where a black baker in Trinidad tells his success story; and finally in 'A Flag on the Island' (1965), which purports to be an American's view of the past and present of a Caribbean island. Unsurprisingly, the stories in the third category were all written in the 1960s despite their random appearance in the collection.

The first-person narratives in 'A Christmas Story' and 'The Baker's Story' are presented in voices which define themselves as specific Trinidadian types: the Trinidadian Indian Christian in the former, where the operative term is Christian; and the black Trinidadian baker in the latter, where the operative term is black. The events that occur to these characters, their responses to these events, and their conduct in life are sieved through their all-subsuming self-consciousness of being Christian or black. Arguably, converting to Presbyterianism, as a matter of faith or for the social advantages that being Presbyterian may confer, especially in the midst of a conservative Hindu environment, is a self-defining act which may colour every aspect of the Indian Trinidadian Choonilal's – or Randolph's, as he becomes – engagement with his world. That is what Naipaul conveys in 'A Christmas Story': becoming a Christian in that environment is a defining act which involves a displacement, a wistfulness for things European, and a distaste for his own heritage. It explains the exaggerated, and even agonized, self-definition of being a Christian in Randolph's story:

> As much as by the name Randolph, pleasure was given me by the stately and *clean* – there is no other word for it – rituals sanctioned by my new religion. [...] Such of the unconverted village folk who were energetic enough to be awake and alert at that hour gaped at us as we walked in white procession to our church. And though their admiration was sweet, I must confess that at the same time it filled me with shame to reflect that not long before I too formed part of the gaping crowd. To walk past their gaze was peculiarly painful to me, for I, more perhaps than anyone in that slow and stately procession, *knew* – and by my silence had for nearly eighteen years condoned – the practices those people indulged in in the name of religion. (*FI* 26)

Similarly (though more tenuously), it is perhaps understandable that the black baker would begin his story with the following words:

> Look at me. Black as the Ace of Spades, and ugly to match. Nobody looking at me would believe they looking at one of the richest men in this city of Port-of-Spain. (*FI* 111)

and actually carry on in that vein all through. The idea is probably that being black, especially, like this baker, as an apprentice in a Chinese bakery initially and later following a profession which is not associated with black people, heightens racial self-awareness. Perhaps it also naturalizes racial self-hatred: note that he doesn't merely announce himself as black but 'ugly to match'. Naipaul's cultural critique of Caribbean society's internal meaninglessness and penchant for looking outwards, of suffering from a constant colonial anxiety of displacement, can 'explain' the subsuming self-awareness of these Trinidadian *types*. The overall effect of these stories, at any rate, is of presenting not the subjectivity of different world-views, but the objectivity of the narrators who ostensibly speak. The reader is not really invited to look at the world as a black or Christian Trinidadian might, but to look at these obsessively self-consciously black or Christian Trinidadian characters who happen to speak. The very style of their speech invites appraisal of them rather than an entry into their worlds: the ponderous semi-biblical style of Randolph's speech, and the deliberate distribution of colloquialisms in the black baker's speech, render the written texts of their narratives that much more opaque.

This provides a useful contrast to the long title story which also belongs to this category. It was apparently commissioned by a film company and required a treatment of island themes, hence the subtitle, 'A Fantasy for a Small Screen'. The fantasy element is laboured in the story by the sometimes hallucinatory and surreal and occasionally nostalgic view which is presented by the first-person narrator, Frank, an American soldier who had been stationed on the island during the war and returns many years later. The fantasy element fits in ironically with the absurd and all-too-real changes that Frank encounters on his return. The wartime island which Frank had originally visited was a colourful and quaintly Caribbean island inhabited by eccentric and memorable characters: Henry the brothel owner, H. J. Blackwhite the teacher and would-be novelist who wrote romances about English lords and ladies, the preacher who turned insurance agent, and so on. The oddly out-of-place aspirations and activities of these characters were not too odd actually, because it all came together in a carnivalesque fashion:

> On the Tuesday evening, when the streets were full of great figures – Napoleon, Julius Caesar, Richard the Lion-heart: men parading with concentration – Blackwhite was also abroad, dressed like Shakespeare. (*FI* 165)

The island that Frank returns to has clearly lost some of that carnivalesque spirit and quaintness, and in its bid to affirm its own identity has simply succeeded in becoming the sham of a tourist resort with commodified cultural expressions and a real loss of identity. In this, Henry has an MBE and is the owner of a posh hotel and restaurant, H. J. Blackwhite has become established as the native voice and now passes ironically as H. J. B. White, the preacher has become a radio presenter, and so on. As Frank observes:

> Once the island had seemed to me to be flagless. There was the Union Jack of course, but it was a remote affirmation. The island was a floating suspended place to which you brought your own flag if you wanted to. (FI 132)

The title indicates that now a flag has been planted and it is all wrong.

All this is *seen* by Frank. Frank's narrative is strange and disjunctive, leaps about with a dream-like logic, but that's not because Frank is a strange fellow, it's because he encounters the strangeness of change in the Caribbean. Unlike the narrators of 'A Christmas Story' or 'The Baker's Story' Frank's narratorial language, despite its peculiarities, is transparent. It is to be seen through, not looked at. Frank is at best a flickering presence, difficult to pin down or characterize, and certainly not with the simple adjective of a flat type-cast character. Frank provides, so to say, the naturalized extrinsic view which puts the Caribbean island into perspective – frames it and implicitly judges it.

A similar shift of perspectives informs Ralph Singh's account of his life in *The Mimic Men* too. The strange hybridized name, Ralph Singh (actually Ranjit Kripalsingh), is itself indicative of that subtle counterposing of perspectives. It is given as Ralph Singh's autobiographical account. This begins with his early life in the Caribbean island of Isabella, amidst his family and school friends; then describes his move to England, his life in the boarding house run by Lieni, his various sexual adventures, and his eventual marriage to Sandra; delineates his return to Isabella where he establishes himself successfully as a property developer and building contractor, and where he enters politics with his friend Browne and rises to power; accounts for his sudden desertion from his political office in Isabella to return to England, his brief affair with the aristocratic Stella there, and his settling down in the old boarding house (now a hotel) where he begins writing these memoirs. That is the chronologically organized sequence of events – but they are not given chronologically. Ralph Singh's narrative follows the rationale of his writing of it: the memories are committed to paper apparently as they arise, and the act of reading his narrative traverses this sequence of memories in all their haphazardness. In *The Mimic Men* the act of writing and the act of reading merge into an identical unchronological and unlinear process: almost metaphorically the writer and the reader reach a harmonious relationship which is deliberately outside the simple logic of linear narrative and transfer. Ultimately *The Mimic Men* is an explicit enactment of the act of writing, with an implicit understanding of the processive act of reading it therefore becomes available to. Clearly, the schisms in Naipaul's self-consciousness of writing discussed above are healed in this achievement of a harmonized relationship between the process of writing and reading.

In other ways too the schisms are explored further and, so to say, healed: a more composite presentation of cultural perspectives occurs here which clarifies the troubled and equivocal elements of Naipaul's early social critiques of Trinidad. The cultural appraisals which appeared juxtaposed only in a fractured fashion in his Trinidad novels and his English novel, and were in closer proximity in *A Flag on the Island*, actually come together and merge into a single narrative in *The Mimic Men*. The make-belief, passive and essentially hollow Caribbean society of his early novels and the alienated but coherent and active England of *Mr Stone and the Knights Companion* meet in the stark comparative cultural appraisals of *The Mimic Men*. The title underlines the strengthening of Naipaul's perspective both of the Caribbean and of England: the mimic and the mimicked are brought together.

The contrast and complementarity of mimic and mimicked is worked into the novel carefully through a continuous series of counterpoints, too numerous to be listed here. A useful example may suffice to make the point: consider the nature of Ralph's contribution to Caribbean politics. Both Ralph's father and Ralph are political leaders: the former inspires an indigenous mystical grass-roots movement which proves to be ineffective and peters out; while the latter brings a few shallow images (faintly left-leaning, as the title of their international paper, *The Socialist*, suggests) into the political arena which prove to be infinitely more effective. The father's movement, clearly one of the people of Isabella (a 'lower-class movement' is how it is described), is summarized in the following fashion:

> Movements like my father's – without that purpose which might have turned them into true revolutions – expressed despair but were at the same time positive. They generated anger in people who thought they were too dispirited even for that; they generated comradeship. Above all, they generated disorder where previously everyone had deluded himself that there was order. Disorder was drama, and drama was discovered to be a necessary human nutrient. (*MiM* 127)

The indigenous and grass-roots movement in the Caribbean, in other words, rises out of and fills in and recedes into the nullity of Caribbean culture. It is without effective purpose, it expresses despair, it generates disorder, it momentarily hides the lackadaisical spirit of the people, and is as transitory as drama. As against this there are the images presented by Ralph and Browne:

> Consider the stir we made. Consider the peculiar power of my name. Add to this my reputation as a dandy and then the more forbidding reputation as a very young 'Isabella millionaire' who 'worked hard and played hard'. Consider Browne's licensed status as a renegade and romantic, a 'radical', for whose acknowledged gifts our island provided no outlet. See then how, though as individuals we were politically nothing, we supported one another and together appeared as a portent no one could dismiss. Certain ideas overwhelm by their simplicity. In three months – just six issues of the new *Socialist*, its finances and organization regulated by me – we found ourselves at the centre less of a political awakening than a political anxiety, to which it was left to us merely to give direction. (*MiM* 189–90)

A set of clichés – a few hackneyed images from B-grade films and pulp fiction – is ultimately the only effective political means which rouses Isabella. The profound insubstantiality of these images ('politically nothing') and yet their paradoxical success defines the political ethos of Isabella.

The counterpoint to this vision of the nullity and insubstantiality of Caribbean politics is emphasized by the stripping away of clichés and images which occurs only in England. When Ralph Singh sheds his camouflage of being the Isabella political figure, he recedes into an uncomplicated existence in London. London becomes the truth of Ralph Singh while in Isabella he is

31

inevitably a fake. Predictably, when he tires of his mimicry politics, he suddenly deserts Isabella and disappears in London. He goes back to the boarding house in London from where he had reappeared in Isabella with the prospect of financial and political success. Similarly, Browne too emerges from London to his political career in Isabella, though in a less accountable fashion. In a fleeting but telling encounter with Browne in London, one gets the picture of a person who has come into his own – and it is all to do with the peculiar effect of London:

> He was in a hurry, as I have said. But I thought, even from that slight encounter, that London had had an effect on him, as it had had on me. He was lighter and freer than he had been in the sixth form (*MiM* 185).

Put bluntly, the counterpoint of cultural appraisals available in Naipaul's sixties fiction could be presented as follows: Englishness (which can be generalized as Western or First World for the body of Naipaul's writings) provides an occasionally dull and alienating but nevertheless active, self-possessed and affirmative cultural formation; whereas Trinidad, though apparently ebullient and eccentric, is at the core a poor, passive, empty and makeshift culture. It gradually becomes clear that the former has helped Naipaul put the latter into perspective; England throws Trinidad into relief for Naipaul, provides a frame. Naipaul's narratorial perspectives and stylistic features merge comfortably with England and are deliberately distanced from the Caribbean; Naipaul writes with England and at Trinidad; England appears in an expository fashion whereas Trinidad is usually conceived in an evaluative fashion; the English view is naturalized while the Trinidadian view is denaturalized.[2] In different ways this operative counterpoint is extended to other cultural appraisals (primarily of the so-called Third World and more rarely of the so-called First World) later: the patterns recur continuously with changes of emphasis and scope in his later fictional and non-fictional writing. More importantly, it is also given a sort of ideological justification – to discern that the non-fictional writing of the sixties about the Caribbean needs to be taken into account. For that I turn to *The Middle Passage* and *The Loss of El Dorado*.

4

An 'Objective' View of the Caribbean

Naipaul's view of Trinidad (or the Caribbean) as the culture of mimicry and England (or the West) as the mimicked culture is derived from his reading and assimilation of colonial experience and colonial history. *The Middle Passage*, as Naipaul explained in his first foreword, was written as the result of a trip to Trinidad and Tobago in 1960 on a government scholarship and at the suggestion of the then premier of Trinidad, Dr Eric Williams. It describes the author's passage to his home country amongst a motley crowd of tourists and his encounter with would-be West Indian émigres to Britain; his reflections on Trinidad; his explorations into the interior of British Guyana and his encounter with important political figures, particularly Dr. C. B. Jagan; his experiences thereafter in Surinam, Martinique, and Jamaica, and his thoughts about miscellaneous subjects (ranging from history to local languages to Rastafarians); and concludes with an idyllic stay at a luxury hotel in Jamaica called Frenchman's Cove, where all the guests are given whatever they desire. The whole rambling account of the visit is interspersed with 'documentary' evidence of different sorts (usually newspaper cuttings; accounts by other, primarily European, visitors; and historical anecdotes), and the author's (generally damning) views. *The Loss of El Dorado*, on the other hand, is Naipaul's attempt to go back in time – it is an historical account of Trinidad and the surrounding area from 1592 to 1813. It is episodic in structure. The first part is devoted to descriptions of Antonio de Berrio's and Walter Raleigh's fruitless search for El Dorado (the mythical city of gold); then the narrative turns to the establishment of slave trade and plantations. A detailed account of the condition of Trinidad under the oppressive governorship of Picton (when the consolidation and institutionalization of slavery assumed its most grim aspect) follows; then there is an examination of the conflict between Picton and the later-appointed First Commissioner Fullarton (culminating in the trial of Picton's governorship over the Luisa Calderon case – i.e. the torture of a young slave girl to prove a trumped-up theft charge); and finally the historical narrative concludes with the moves towards abolition at the beginning of the nineteenth century and the appearance of the first Chinese indentured labourers. In the course of the above the reader also gets a sense of the rise and fall of revolutionary movements in the Caribbean in the wake of the American war of independence and the French revolution. The narrative is presented as straightforward history; it is erratically referenced, but is attended by a bibliography listing source documents.

Together, the two books present a complete view of Naipaul's reflections on the process and outcome of colonial domination. Clearly, his assessment of this process and outcome is linked to his cultural evaluations of the Caribbean and other contexts: it provides him with a set of ideological values. The question that arises is, of course, what exactly is the link?

There are several interesting points of analysis and evaluation which emerge from *The Middle Passage*. These need to be distinguished and the complex relations between these discerned.

First, all the different cultural contexts which are examined are presented, in keeping with his fictional narratives, as mimicry cultures. These cultures are shown to be subsumed by a sense of the colonizing cultures to which they have been exposed and at the behest of which they have come to exist. The influence of the Dutch on Surinam, for instance, or that of the French in Martinique, is shown to be all-pervasive.

Second, the mimicry is not merely of colonizers and ex-colonizers. The cultural void of the West Indies is also susceptible to dominant cultures – in the case of Trinidad essentially the American. According to Naipaul, modernity in Trinidad, therefore, 'turns out to be the extreme susceptibility of people who are unsure of themselves and, having no taste or style of their own, are eager for instruction' (*MP* 50). This explains the out-of-place impact of American advertising agencies and of Hollywood films, or the crass commercialization that he sees in modern Trinidadian culture (say, in selling calypso to the West). Similarly, Naipaul also realizes that, 'Living in a borrowed culture, the West Indian, more than most, needs writers to tell him who he is and where he stands' (*MP* 73). He asseverates that in this West Indian writers have provided poor examples, usually catering to a false and retrogressive sense of racial and communal pride, and often inspired (as is the case with black writers) by external examples ('American Negro writing'). In discussing the impact of dominant cultures, dominant is variously seen as either an external authentic culture, or a dominant capitalist force (some might say, a neo-imperialist force). In a note to the Penguin edition, Naipaul expresses approval of a review by a New Zealand writer who had described *The Middle Passage* as 'about the problems of a client culture and a client economy' (*MP* 6).

Third, there is a link between the two points made above. It is suggested that the cultural influence of the colonizer is somehow depleted by the impact of so-called dominant cultures. The callousness and brutality of the process of colonization (especially its evolution through slavery) is made trenchantly at several places, but this does not take away from the fact that most West Indian countries as constituted now are the creations of colonization, and the colonizer has provided their *raison d'être*. So, one occasionally finds Naipaul struck with a sense of nostalgia (despite the revulsion at the prejudices implicit therein) for the colonial West Indies of the recent past – often presented through the eyes of colonialist writers like J. A. Froude, Anthony Trollope, Charles Kingsley – and a sense of disappointment and loss in the present. He also clearly sympathizes with some of the critical perceptions of the colonial writers.

Fourth, behind the several levels of mimicry and desire there is also the unavoidable fact of confrontations and clashes between the various racial and cultural groups in the West Indies. Naipaul sees little that is positive in the racially mixed population: in his view the racial and cultural communities do not harmonize, inevitably there is conflict amongst them. More importantly, instead of a synthesized hybridized culture appearing, he encounters cultural and racial conservatism, which is matched by the absurdity of their displacement from their origins. Naipaul is therefore equally scathing about the insular and conservative Indian Trinidadians, of the white expatriates' lack of intellectuality and materialism, of the black community's racial self-assertion or pan-Africanism, of the eccentricity of the Rastafarians' mystical-liberal creed, and of Caribbean neo-nationalisms.

Fifth, despite the general pessimism, Naipaul does have his moments of admiration for affirmative and progressive phenomena in these countries, though these are always under threat. Thus, he sees in the calypso something authentically Trinidadian and admires its carnivalesque spontaneous spirit (though threatened by commercialization); he is impressed by Dr Jagan's political energy in British Guyana (and overwhelmed by the enormity of the pettiness and indolence which opposes him); and he is favourably struck by the quality of Mr Eersel's translation of Wyatt's poem into Negro English in Surinam.

Sixth, there are moments when the cultures he looks at seem to become self-contained in stereotypes which are not simply explicable in terms of mimicry or displacement: Port of Spain is described as the loudest place he knows, for instance, and the Guyanese as the most lackadaisical.

Seventh, and finally, Naipaul paradoxically speaks of, and conducts his criticism of, all these contexts from an immense and unenunciated distance and yet with unmistakable rage. He acknowledges his past in Trinidad and speaks of the need to face up to it, but does so with the air of an informed outsider, though a cynical and bitter one. All the people he meets are met with a self-consciousness of his outside position. But it is difficult to gauge what this outside position is, and what values he brings with him to explain his bitterness. Later, in *The Enigma of Arrival* he was to describe his approach to *The Middle Passage* in the following words:

> I knew, and was glamoured by the idea of the metropolitan traveller, the man starting from Europe. It was the only kind of model I had; but – as a colonial among colonials who were very close to me – I could not be that kind of traveller, even though I might share that traveller's education and culture and have his feeling for adventure.

Especially I was aware of not having a metropolitan audience to 'report back' to. The fight between my idea of the glamour of the traveller-writer and the rawness of my nerves as a colonial travelling among colonials made for difficult writing. (*EA* 140).

One suspects that the distance of his appraisal arises from his sense of sharing the European 'traveller's education and culture' (values?), and his bitterness from sharing at some inescapable level what is condemned from that perspective. The latter is not only cultural critique, but bitterness at his own affiliations. In other words, the values are Eurocentric, but the person who willingly espouses them cannot be that without denying himself. To some extent *The Middle Passage* expresses the agony of this self-denial.

So what does all that add up to? To a certain degree that would always be a moot question. The answer would depend on how any reader of Naipaul's work chooses to bring together the above observations. A few suggestive points can, however, be tentatively made at this stage. It is evident that the counterpoint of mimic cultures and mimicked cultures used to understand some of Naipaul's early fiction is also a sustainable frame for Naipaul's non-fictional writing about the Caribbean. This counterpoint is not merely a simplistic description of the relationship of colonizer and colonized. A far more complex set of inter-relations are implicit in the mimic-mimicked counterpoint. And yet an apprehension of the colonial process and ideology is at the heart of it. The colonial process and ideology is not simply the backdrop to Naipaul's observations and the origin of the states of affairs that he examines; it is also contained in his vision and constituted in his own psyche. The colonial experience is not simply a determinative element in the cultural vistas before Naipaul (these cultural vistas are complex formations which are based on that experience and its aftermath); the colonial experience is central because its inbuilt in Naipaul's thinking and aspirations as a writer. The preoccupation with colonial experience is a self-reflexive preoccupation: it reflects Naipaul's colonized mind. This point will, I hope, get gradually clarified below.

Predictably, a large part of Naipaul's subsequent writings on the theme try to either evade this recognition or else externalize this recognition. *The Loss of El Dorado* is an attempt at evasion, which is nevertheless a disclosure of the self-reflexive colonial psyche. This is probably the only book in which Naipaul tries to efface the creative persona as completely as possible: it is presented with all the security of a historical narrative in which everything can be referred to documentary evidence. Naipaul stresses the narratorial self-effacement and historical authenticity of his effort in the Postscript of *The Loss of El Dorado*:

> This narrative was structured mainly from documents – originals, copies, printed – in the British Museum, the Public Record Office, London, and the London Library. Most of the translations are my own. Dialogue occurs as dialogue in the sources. (*LED* 379)

Naipaul allows himself no more than the translator's privileges. But historical narrative does not necessarily involve self-effacement. When Naipaul reconsidered his book in retrospective, as he did in a substantial section of *The Enigma of Arrival*, it turned out to be exactly what it doesn't appear to be in the first instance – a writer's attempt to come to grips with and feel reconciled to his own colonial psyche. Naipaul endeavours to live comfortably with his colonized mind, and when he reflected on *The Loss of El Dorado* later he felt he had achieved exactly that:

> Ever since I had begun to identify my subjects I had hoped to arrive, in a book, at a synthesis of the worlds and cultures that made me. The other way of writing, the separation of one world from the other, was easier, but I felt it false to the nature of my experience. I felt in this history I had made such a synthesis. (*EA* 144)

Even later, in the already quoted *Face to Face* interview with Jeremy Isaacs in 1994, Naipaul expressed his regret at the unnecessary attempt at self-effacement in this book.

As I have mentioned above, historical writing does not necessarily entail self-effacement, and Naipaul's history was recognized by critics from the beginning[1] to be less objective reportage than he had pretended. Inevitably, a historian reconstructs the past in the light of, and within the constraints of, the present. The degree of research, the selection of material, the linking of facts, and of course the conclusions drawn are each indicative of interpretive acts. In the *Loss of El Dorado* each of these provide interesting insights into Naipaul's approach and mind-set.

It could be noted, for instance, that the documentary evidence that Naipaul relies on is entirely dependent on the colonial entrepreneurs' testimonies. The actual and fantasy-woven encounters with the land and its inhabitants (Columbus, Berrio and others) is rendered in detail. But there is no attempt to provide a context for this land and its inhabitants outside the colonial entrepreneurs' view, though anthropological and socio-historical research in the area wasn't unknown[2] – and certainly should be conducted in a historical exposition of this nature. The only index of a view of the land that is opposed (albeit rarely) to the documentary sources is from Naipaul's own memory. The writer and the documentary sources are actually engaged in a complicitous relationship from the beginning of the book. As a result the book becomes largely a record of the colonizer's passion, energy, arrogance and bewilderment; the colonial view subsumes the land and its inhabitants, reduces them to a shadowy and entirely instrumental presence, maintains the colonizers' hierarchical self-esteem, and their sense of their own humanity (not humaneness, quite the opposite) as against the intangibility of those who are invaded. It is a familiar counterpoint seen in the earliest writings of Naipaul: the native's passivity is filled in by the European's adventurousness (which is shown to be brutal and self-serving and yet vital).

This counterpoint of passivity–activity gets translated soon to the most obvious thematic preoccupation of the book, the institution of slavery. Necessarily, any attempt to come to grips with the institution of slavery has to examine the rules and modes of subjection involved. Naipaul does this faithfully: he starts with the relatively humane laws relating to slaves in Port of Spain in 1790 (where 'The slave remained an individual, not totally outcast', *LED* 133), and moves on to a searing description of the gradual dehumanization and degradation of slaves under Picton (exemplified in detailed descriptions of the tortures and mutilations of slaves in Vallot's prison), and of slaves coming to be used as bodies which can receive chastisement for their masters by proxy (Picton is shown to habitually 'get at' his white enemies and rivals 'through their negroes'). To see the extent to which the institution of slavery dehumanizes and degrades the slave, renders the slave passive and voiceless, no more than chattel, is, of course, the most damning indictment of slavery.

This Naipaul recounts (as I have said) faithfully.

But there is another side to Naipaul's view of slavery – his perspective of slave rebellion and resistance. He deals in some detail with two important instances of slave rebellion (apart from numerous incidents of mass poisoning). Naipaul describes the wave of slave rebellions (or black rebellions) in the wake of the French revolution of 1789, especially the ill-fated one in Trinidad; and he recounts the underground slave organizations ('kingdoms') which were investigated and suppressed from 1805 in Port of Spain. The first is briefly summarized in the following:

> Negroes wore the tricolour cockade and sang the *Marseillaise*. It was part of the French absurdity: the slave revolt was not wholly a slave revolt, the race war was not wholly a race war. All the local hatreds were entangled with the revolutionary politics of France. Paris supplied each side with the same simple vocabulary of revolution, words that were like part of the drama and promise: even the pretty climatic names – *germinal, brumaire* – of a new calender of the North. (*LED* 139)

The latter is depicted as a somewhat grotesque fantasy of the night *(negro,* after all), ineffective and ludicrous:

> It came out in the Council chamber as a confused Negro story, unrelated fragments of an extended, confused fantasy. Between the curfew and sunrise these kings and courtiers, generals and judges, so many suffering from sores, visited and exchanged courtesies. They blessed, they punished. France, England and Africa, the plantations themselves, the church and the Council provided the rituals, the titles, the ceremonies of power. (*LED* 295)

It is not the 'real thing', appears to be Naipaul's inference. His tendency to declare mimicry and search for some mysterious authenticity resurfaces. The implication is clear: the passivity of the slaves (blacks) had become endemic – even their resistance was a passively play-acted and incoherent gesture.

Yet it may be justifiably maintained that these instances of rebellion and subversion were not simply play-acting: they represented something extraordinary and unthinkably courageous given the circumstances in which they were conceived. And the French revolutionary ideas which inspired the former, and the mixed organizational modes and ritual practices assumed in the latter, were neither a betrayal of something authentic nor ultimately a corrupt submission to the colonizer – they were the only modes of resistance conceivable in that context. To consider the notion of organized mass uprising and utopian socialist and communist revolutionary ideas which emerged from the French revolution, along with the tactics of underground organization connected to these, to be culture-specific and race-specific is a peculiarly conservative asseveration. It is only possible to maintain that if the Manichean colonial black-and-white vision is so ingrained that any hybridized and creolized phenomenon seems to be somehow tainted.[3] The obvious contrast of Naipaul's history in this regard (and it seems to me that Naipaul deliberately plays up this contrast) to the most famous polemical historical account of slave rebellion in the wake of the French revolution hardly needs to be mentioned. C. L. R. James's account of the only successful slave rebellion in history, which led to the formation of the black republic of Haiti, in *The Black Jacobins: Toussaint L'Ouverture and the San Domingo Revolution* (1938)[4] must inevitably be evoked here.[5] James's penchant for focusing on the hero-figure may be a jot excessive, and the Marxist analysis (and especially the link to the African situation in the final pages) a bit tenuous, but the depth of political and ideological perception is incomparably more compelling. The comparison clarifies the outcome of Naipaul's history. It reveals what *The Middle Passage* had already revealed. Naipaul's modes of cultural engagement and assessment are held together by his understanding of the process and experience of colonization; and the most significant feature of this understanding is not (as he has sometimes claimed) so much the harsh 'truth-telling' it involves as the revelation of the writer's black-and-white colonial psyche.

What is valuable about Naipaul's writings thereafter, as I demonstrate below, is his unflinching and unembarrassed revelation of, and confrontation with, himself.

5

Writing About Blackness

In the decade following the sixties Naipaul's writings show a change in focus. Until that point the historical descriptions and cultural critiques of colonized (or ex-colonized) contexts had been conducted in terms of a colonizer–colonized counterpoint (active–passive, authentic–parodic etc.); and this was paradoxically reflective, as I have said, of the writer's black-and-white colonial psyche. Inevitably, all the writings so far had, despite carefully deployed distanciation techniques and the affectation of objective narrative, some autobiographical investment. The writing of historical and cultural contexts was always also an exposition on the writer's roots – intertwined within the Caribbean context, extended to the migratory placement in England, and stretched back ultimately to the peculiarities of the Hindu Trinidadian community and its Indian origins (a discussion of Naipaul's Indian writings comes later in this study). The writings of the seventies gradually exorcize the obvious autobiographical investment in Naipaul's creative and critical preoccupations. The cultural critique and historical descriptions which had also been a charting of the self are gradually dislocated from their obvious territory (the Caribbean, England, India), and extended to a more cosmopolitan arena. The Caribbean island that appears in *Guerrillas* (1975) is scarcely recognizable as the Caribbean islands Naipaul had written about before. The expatriate Hindu Trinidadian consciousness which was manifest in most of the earlier books is carefully removed: instead the island of *Guerrillas* is seen through the expatriate perspective of Roche (an activist in South Africa, who had suffered at the hands of the apartheid regime), the naive English adventuress Jane, the Black Power activist Jimmy Ahmad, the black politician and power-broker Meredith, and the white expatriate settler Harry. Centre-stage in this novel is the politics of the Black Power movement associated with Michael X in Trinidad, about which Naipaul had written a substantial essay (an account of the actual events which inspired *Guerrillas*) entitled 'Michael X and the Black Power Killings in Trinidad'. The latter was published in a collection of essays entitled *'The Return of Eva Perón' with 'The Killings in Trinidad'* (1980). Interestingly the other essays in this collection, written primarily between 1972 and 1975 (as the author states in the preface), attest to the more cosmopolitan arena Naipaul was reaching towards at this stage. The title essay, 'The Return of Eva Perón', describes the resurgence of Peronism and the potency of the myth of Evita Perón in Argentina; and the two final essays, 'A New King for the Congo: Mobutu and the Nihilism of Africa' and 'Conrad's Darkness', take Naipaul's readers to his view of Africa.

In the seventies, in fact, Africa and the black race became a significant focus for Naipaul's creative and critical energies. *Guerrillas* is to some extent ironically sieved through Roche's experiences in South Africa and hinges on an understanding of the Black Power movement which originated in the United States of America (associated primarily with Malcolm X) and gravitated towards Africa. It was preceded by the novella *In a Free State* (which appeared under that title along with two other stories in 1971), set in an unnamed African country; and was followed by *A Bend in the River* (1979), a transparent fictionalization of Naipaul's vision of Mobutu Sese Seko's Zaire. Naipaul's travel diary of Zaire – a brief and unorganized collection of notes – was also published in a limited edition of 330 copies as *A Congo Diary* (1980). And finally, in *Finding the Centre* (1984), one finds another African travel diary (of the Ivory Coast), 'The Crocodiles of Yamoussoukro', appended to the autobiographical essay entitled 'Prologue to an Autobiography' – ostensibly as a demonstration of the writer's creative skills, the development of which had been charted in the autobiographical essay.

Despite the change of focus in Naipaul's creative and critical preoccupations (the attempt to engage with a more cosmopolitan arena, with a focus on Africa), and the careful deletion of any obvious autobiographical setting, there remains an unmissable continuity between these and his earlier books. Arguably, the self-reflexive colonial psyche is constant: its metaphoric black-and-whiteness gets translated to actual images of blackness and whiteness; these books demonstrate the exacerbation of Naipaul's racialized colonial consciousness within his cultural critiques.

The charges that Naipaul brings against the Black Power movement as embodied in Michael X (or Abdul Malik) and his Christina Gardens commune in Trinidad in his essay 'Michael X and the Black Power Killings in Trinidad' follow a by-now familiar pattern:

> He was the X, the militant, the man threatening the fire next time; he was also the dope peddler, the pimp. He was everybody's Negro, and not too Negroid [Michael X was half white]. He had two ideas of his own. One was that the West Indian High Commissions in London paid too little attention to their nationals. The other, more bizarre, was that the uniform of the Trinidad police should be changed; and this was less an idea than an obsession. Everything else was borrowed, every attitude, every statement: from the adoption of the X and the conversion to Islam, down to the criticism of white liberals ('destroying the black man') and the black bourgeois ('they don't know the man from the ghetto'). He was the total 1960s Negro, in a London setting; and his very absence of originality, his plasticity, his ability to give people the kind of Negro they wanted, made him acceptable to journalists. (*REP* 29)

In other words, Michael X's contribution to the Black Power movement had all the deficiencies of colonial politics and culture in general as Naipaul saw it. It lacked authenticity, its conceptual framework and vocabulary were borrowed and superficial. There is the usual positing of the implied and authentic sources of these borrowings. Naipaul doesn't spell this out, but the sources are indicated clearly enough, and they break down into two sorts. The one that Naipaul addresses most explicitly in the essay is the one that he identifies with Western liberalism and revolutionary socialism (grounded in the white colonizer's cultures): that is, where Michael X's communism and its vocabulary derive from. Naipaul systematically denigrates Michael X's appropriations from this source: his alleged knowledge of Western literature and political philosophy is shown to be little more than pretension; his literacy is brought into question (Naipaul acidly highlights the poor grammar in Michael X's writings); his ideas are constantly restated to make them seem patently absurd (note the comment on Michael X's 'two ideas of his own'); and he is reduced to little more than a carnivalesque fool. The other source, which Naipaul gestures towards clearly in the above quotation but doesn't discuss at any length, is the civil liberties and Black Power movement in the United States in the sixties.[1] The antisocial background of the ghetto black, the eschewing of the slave name (replaced by X), the association with Islam, the critical positions with regard to white liberals and black bourgeoisie, are, of course, all reminiscent of Malcolm X – and all enumerated and elucidated in his famous autobiography.[2] 'The fire next time' recalls the black American writer James Baldwin's essay (in the form of a letter to his nephew) which was published under that title.[3]

At any rate, Naipaul overplays the former and underplays the latter, and the denunciation of Michael X and the Black Power movement in Trinidad follows accordingly. It is, for Naipaul, another failure of authenticity in colonized cultures – and in the process of making that point he seems to refrain from any evaluation of the authentic roots of Black Power in the United States by simply asserting that race is irrelevant in Trinidad:

> Malik's career proves how much of Black Power – away from its United States source – is jargon, how much a sentimental hoax. In a place like Trinidad, racial redemption is as irrelevant for the Negro as for everybody else. It obscures the problems of a small independent country with a lopsided economy, the problems of a fully 'consumer' society that is yet technologically untrained and without the independent means to comprehend the deficiency. It perpetuates the negative, colonial politics of protest. (*REP* 70)

One may feel mystified by the quotation marks around 'consumer', but the point is reasonably clear: the explanation is, as I have mentioned already, in keeping with Naipaul's views as elaborated in his early writings.

What remains comparatively inexplicable, and what emerges as a disturbingly new feature of Naipaul's critical-creative world, is the violence. In the essay in question Naipaul dwells on the details of the murders that were committed by bodyguard Steve Yeates and one Hakim Jamal at the Christina Gardens commune, possibly at the instance of Michael X – especially that of Jamal's English lover, Gale Ann Benson. Naipaul's remorselessly understated description of the details naturally shock by their brutality, but it is more the tone with which Naipaul undertakes to do this which may rouse interest. The gratuitous violence which Naipaul describes is a new feature of his critical-creative world; the cultural critique he offers therein is familiar but the stark violence is new. What is interesting about Naipaul's tone is that it deals with this shocking and, in some sense, new phenomenon with a complete lack of curiosity. By doing so he takes the mystery away from the killings in the commune, and he gives the impression that no explanations are necessary for the violence because it is self-evident and completely understandable in its context. It is simply a repugnant symptom of the sickness in the Michael X and Black Power movement. The sickness, Naipaul suggests, is the distortion of racial conflict; that is why the murder of the white Gale Ann Benson assumes metaphoric proportions, and the title simply labels the murders 'the Black Power Murders'. But that still leaves a question: why is violence more endemic in the Black Power phenomenon than it is in the other forms of colonial cultural vacuity that Naipaul had examined before? No clear answer is offered in the essay (just the uncurious attitude and the tacit agreement that he understands it and is disgusted by it), but one may hope to find a clue in Naipaul's extended fictionalized treatment of these murders in his novel *Guerrillas*.

There are two strands to *Guerrillas*. One of the strands is inhabited by Roche (with a past of torture in South Africa and a journalistic book about his experiences there, currently employed by a large multinational company on the island) and Jane (his lover and former literary agent, who joins him on the island), and their circle – mainly Harry, a colleague of Roche's, and Meredith, a government man and ruthless political analyst on the radio. The other strand is occupied by the commune at Thrushcross Grange, led by the self-promoting, self-serving and dangerous Jimmy Ahmad (half-Chinese and half-black), followed by a group of young delinquents (especially his 'queer' lover Bryant), and with a breakaway member, Stephens (who has his own gang), somewhere on the fringe. Much of the book is devoted to delineating the two strands. On the one hand, the relationship of Jane and Roche (which gradually disintegrates) is examined, the preoccupations of their circle and their home life are described; on the other hand the background of Jimmy Ahmad (not unlike Michael X) and his self-obsessed masochistic fantasy world is shown, along with that of the agonized and lonely Bryant. The occupants of both strands are dogged by a sense of their own insubstantiality and of futility: this is highlighted particularly in the discussions of the Roche circle at parties, in Jimmy's fantasy letters, and finally in the radio interview of Roche by Meredith. The links between the two strands form the substance of the book. Roche has an interest in Jimmy and his commune for some vague business reason. Jimmy's commune and Stephens's gang stage an uprising against the government (Meredith is a minister in it), which is only quelled with the assistance of American Marines – it finishes Jimmy's political career, makes a scapegoat of Roche, and re-establishes the power of the alliance between government and American multinational. And there is the link between Jimmy and Jane: in their second meeting Jane becomes Jimmy's lover, and in their third meeting Jimmy rapes and sodomizes her, and then, in a bizarre bonding ritual with Bryant, murders her.

The slippages between the account of the 'Black Power murders' in the essay and the fictionalized account in *Guerrillas* are worth noting. There is a wider background involved in the fictionalized account: an evocation of post-colonial superficiality and its corrupt power politics. The violence of *Guerrillas* derives from this entire background more explicitly than in Naipaul's earlier books on similar themes – it is not absurd and amusing any longer, just violent. But it goes further than that. Within that general violence, there is the peculiar perversity of Jimmy's violence. Unlike Michael X, Jimmy is the result of more intractable racial miscegenation: half-Chinese half-black, not as simply comprehended as the 'mulatto' Michael X. Jimmy's fantasy letters are demonstrative of this complex and curious racial fixation. But it goes further even than that. Unlike anything in the 'Black Power murders' the racial fixation is linked with Naipaul's fraught perception of perverse sexuality. Jimmy's fantasy letters are sexual fantasies. There is a not-too-covert homophobic air in the description of the Bryant–Jimmy relationship. The act of buggery is brought in: interestingly the other reference to buggery that one finds in Naipaul's writings appears in his essay on Argentina, 'The Return of Eva Perón':

The act of straight sex, easily bought, is of no great moment to the macho. His conquest of a woman is complete only when he has buggered her. This is what the woman has it in her power to deny; this is what the brothel game is about, the passionless Latin adventure that begins with talk about *amor*. *La ture en el culo*, I've had her in the arse: this is how the macho reports victory to his circle, or dismisses a desertion. (*REP* 155)

Out of this mixture of racial fixation and sexual perversion emerges Naipaul's explanation of the ultimate act of violence (removed from the general political violence of post-colonial contexts) in *Guerrillas* (and by implication of the Black Power movement). The explanation for Jimmy's committing the murder is clarified in a final fantasy sequence at the moment of committing the murder:

The world cleared up, time defined itself. He was himself, in a stone room, full of incense, with white coffins on stone shelves, where dead women lay without being dead among white lilies. A woman sat up in her stone coffin; the lilies tumbled off her. She was Sudanese, like those he had seen in London: he could tell from her fine white cotton dress, her pallid brown skin and the healed slashes on her cheeks. She had the wanton face, the leer, the degraded mouth of a French prostitute he had seen in a pornographic photograph at school, sitting clothed with her skirt pulled up, her legs open, her great hairiness exposed. She sat up in her roughly chiselled coffin, leering, the lilies falling off her, and she said, holding out her hand, 'Nigger, give me a dollar'. (*BR* 244)

The racial fixation and perverse sexuality go behind the obvious black–white conflict (obvious white symbols like coffins and lilies, the white dress, French prostitutes, London), derive from some deeper racial memory. Jane's whiteness is irrelevant at the moment of the murder; Jimmy's (and Bryant's) violence derives from a deeper racial and cultural masochism – the woman is Sudanese (Jimmy's mother was black), she beckons to a 'nigger', and Jimmy's and Bryant's violence is probably a dark African thing, something purely black.

But why is Jimmy made half-Chinese? That remains a mystery: but it seems reasonably clear that he asserts his blackness (a bonding with Bryant, the masochistic buggery, killing Sudanese women) by murder, possibly all the more emphatically because of his mixed blood. And at this point the reader may recall that the black rationalist in the book, Meredith, had also earlier spoken of the natural 'queer' phase and expressed some sort of sexual fascination with hair (in fact the hair in Jimmy's mother's armpits) – Meredith, despite his sophistication and intelligence, is not entirely unlike Jimmy.

Naipaul's perception of blackness harks back to Africa and the violence therein. Naipaul had already written his novella set in Africa, *In a Free State* (1971), and was to publish *A Bend in the River* (1979) soon after, along with his Zaire and Ivory Coast travel diaries. *In a Free State* describes a cross-country drive by two English expatriates, Bobby and Linda, in an African country on the brink of civil war (a contest of power between a president and a king, representing different tribal interests). In the course of the narrative Africans make cameo appearances, always inscrutable and incoherent and subversive and dangerous. Bobby tries to pick up a young Zulu man from a bar who spits in his face; the travellers come across and occasionally give lifts to threatening African men; they meet peculiarly incoherent and uncooperative African gas station attendants; they put up with a white colonial officer from the past and his African menial, Peter, who will clearly murder his master some day; and finally, Bobby gets roughed up for no apparent reason by a group of African soldiers, whose only conversation seems to consist in repeating what Bobby says in a parrot-like parody. *A Bend in the River* details the experiences of Salim (in his voice), an African of Indian origin, who sets up a shop at a town on the 'river' which had recently been torn by civil war. The novel describes his acquaintances in the town: his family slave, Metty, who joins him there; a young African man, Ferdinand (the son of one of his customers, Zabeth), whose guardianship he reluctantly assumes; the other Indian businessman in the town, Mahesh, and his wife, Shoba; his high-flying friend, Indar; the foreign Africanist, Raymond, and his wife, Yvette (later Salim's lover); the teacher and amateur Africanist, Father Huismans, who gets mysteriously murdered. Some space is devoted to Salim's background and reminiscences – particularly the formative influence of a family friend, Nazruddin, who eventually ends up in London. All these people characteristically (with the exception of Nazruddin, who typically gets away to England) lead unfulfilled lives. And the novel describes the

are shown to be simply inexplicable and irrational, usually adopting a transparent façade with dark depths behind. Peter in *In a Free State* fits the pattern; Ferdinand (the fictional African given the most space) in *A Bend in the River* assumes, as Salim realizes, different roles as and when these suit him and never quite gives himself away; Djédjé in 'The Crocodiles of Yamoussoukro' goes 'wild'. What is interesting about these portrayals is that they are fairly similar to the kind of superficial play-acting that Naipaul had observed in other post-colonial cultures (in the Caribbean, in India) already, but in the case of Africans this doesn't simply hide an essential vacuousness. Most of the other post-colonial peoples and cultures he had written about were condemned by their mimic nature because there was nothing behind the mimicry. But behind the mimicry of the Africans there is something: there is (and this brings us back to the blackness of Michael X or Jimmy Ahmad) a violent and primitive and ritualistic African psyche behind the mimicry. Violent and barbaric rituals and customs surface like revelations from Africa for Naipaul: the killing of babies to honour chieftains, the potent symbolism of Mobutu's sceptre, and so on. Most tellingly, in 'The Crocodiles of Yamoussoukro', 'The crocodile ritual – speaking of a power issuing from the earth itself – was part of the night, endlessly undoing the reality of the day' (*FC* 162). One of the important motifs of *A Bend in the River* is that the patch of civilization that is personified in the township is surrounded by bush and could be subsumed by bush again, indeed seems fated to. In *In a Free State* gradually the wilderness of the landscape presses in on all attempts at civilization and threatens to overpower Linda and Bobby. The violence that pervades the air of Naipaul's Africa is not an explicable violence: it derives from something archetypally African, something that is essentially and irremediably primeval in Africa, something (so to say) purely black. In a sense, in offering this perspective Naipaul does go beyond Conrad. For Conrad the African primitivity and violence did expand out of Africa to symbolize something within imperial Western cultures themselves. As Naipaul says in 'A New King for the Congo', for Conrad the ultimate horror of *The Heart of Darkness* was the lapse of Kurtz (the most promising agent of the 'civilising mission' of imperialism), whereas for Naipaul:

the man with the 'inconceivable mystery of a soul that knew no restraint, no faith and no fear' was black, and not white; and he had been maddened not by contact with wilderness and primitivism, but with the civilization established by those pioneers who lie on Mont Ngaliema, above the Kinshasa rapids. (*REP* 196)

The quotation, of course, applies specifically to Mobutu, but as he makes clear at every opportunity Mobutu represents for him a quintessentially African phenomenon.

To reiterate here that Naipaul's writings about Africa and the Black Power movement are to a large extent reflexive of the writer's black-and-white colonial psyche (with black-and-white exacerbated to a racialized consciousness) is probably supererogatory – that is corollary to the above observations. However, it may be worth recalling at this point (as Naipaul's critics have occasionally mentioned, and as Naipaul has asserted in interviews himself) that there is an objective basis to Naipaul's sentiments. Recent history of a large number of African countries has been remarkably violent. The scenarios of civil war and internecine conflict, the brutal and unnecessary bloodshed, that Naipaul evokes in his descriptions of Africa, would strike a chord with many observers of African affairs and Africans who have lived through similar events. Few would have any quarrel with that aspect of Naipaul's African writings; it is the implicit analysis, with its tenuous sociological basis, which some readers would have reservations about.

6

Filling Gaps

Breaking the more or less chronological order here (I have so far disregarded the books on India and Islamic countries that were written between the sixties and the eighties, but do come to these later), I move on to three books published by Naipaul more recently: *The Enigma of Arrival* (1987), *A Turn in the South* (1989), and *A Way in the World* (1994). These, it seems to be generally agreed, present Naipaul's mature reflections on issues that have preoccupied him consistently from his earliest literary efforts. The three books in question can be seen to fit in systematically with the three areas that the present study has touched on already. *The Enigma of Arrival* arguably substantiates Naipaul's apprehension of England and his self-placement in relation to England (the mimicked culture, to which and within which Naipaul, so to say, arrives); *A Turn in the South* revisits and confronts the issue of racialized thinking (writing about blackness and whiteness) in the context of the southern United States (the 'authentic' source of black civil rights and Black Power movements); *A Way in the World* returns to reflections on colonial and post-colonial history and the Caribbean. These books seem to me to be linked by their sense of retrospection, and by their self-conscious revisiting of themes which Naipaul had dealt with before. The return to previously discussed themes is not, however, merely a reiteration of observations Naipaul had made already. These books indicate an advance on his previous observations, usually by addressing the gaps and omissions which had been manifest in his earlier writings.

The Enigma of Arrival, scrupulously subtitled *A Novel*, is unambiguously presented as an autobiographical narrative: descriptions of the writer's period of residence in a village near Salisbury, an isolated pensive time, intermittently give way to reflections on the writer's past (in Trinidad, of course, and in England, and in all the other places he had visited) and creative efforts. The juxtaposition of the form of the novel with barely fictionalized autobiography is deliberate: for Naipaul both, it seems to be suggested, are made and apprehended in a continuous fashion. Naipaul's life self-consciously flows into his creative work and vice versa. The book largely elucidates what arrival (in a physical sense, and in a metaphorical sense of reaching self-understanding) in England has meant for the writer. Different levels of juxtaposition enable this elucidation: the juxtaposition of the cosmopolitan writer in the rural landscape of Wiltshire; of the writer's colonial past and the colonizer's heritage; of the writer's past as a struggling writer and his present position as an established writer; of the writer's Trinidadian roots and his sense of belonging to England; and, at the broadest level, of the writer as an individual and the social contexts he inhabits.

The Enigma of Arrival allows for a concretization of these juxtapositions to occur by narrowing down the world within which the writer is placed: the rural community of Salisbury. The writer's understanding of himself is put into perspective by delineating the small group of people amongst whom he finds himself. The latter include mainly the writer's landlord (and lord of the manor); the landlord's estate manager, Mr Phillips, and his wife; the local cab-hire man, Bray; the gardener, Pitton; and the writer's neighbour, Jack. Members of these characters' families and other visitors drift in and out of the narrative to complete the sense of community. The affiliations with and sympathies for these characters that the writer forms substantiate him. He sees some of them as archetypal characters in the English rural heritage: for instance, the Phillipses, though actually outsiders, appear to him to be typical estate managers; and Pitton becomes for him the survivor (though he wasn't actually so) of a group of twelve gardeners who had worked the manor ground in its heyday. And there are two landowners (the commoner, Jack, and the lord of the manor), who, to the writer's mind, represent the community as a whole and rural English heritage in general. Living in their midst, and observing the life of the community, the writer gradually realizes both the continuity (detailed descriptions of the eternal landscape come

55

in here) and the decay (the fact that the estate gradually disintegrates, with Mr Phillips's death and Pitton's dismissal) therein.

In the process of delineating this the writer gradually reaches a sort of self-understanding and realizes what 'arrival' has meant for him. This occurs in several ways which are given here point by point. One, the writer tries to place himself with regard to the characters listed above – especially the two representative landowners, with both of whom he has only the most distant relationships (he describes his fleeting encounters with Jack and the landlord). The writer sees himself as the opposite of both, and yet finds a sort of synthesis of opposites in their present coexistence. Jack is seen as the land-bound and fulfilled farmer as opposed to the globe-trotting and also fulfilled writer: they meet in their feeling of being satiated within the Salisbury landscape. The writer's self-appraisal, in relation to the landlord is more revealing:

> So I felt in tune with what I saw or thought I saw at the manor; I felt in myself the same spirit of withdrawal. And though I knew that men might arrive at similar states or attitudes for dissimilar reasons and by different routes, and as men might even be incompatible, I felt at one with my landlord.
>
> Privilege lay between us. But I had an intimation that it worked against him. Whatever my spiritual state at the moment of arrival, I knew I would have to save myself and look for health; I knew I would have to act at some time. His privilege – his house, his staff, his income, the acres he could look out at every day and knew to be his – this privilege could press him down into himself, into non-doing and nullity.
>
> So though we had started at opposite ends of empire and privilege, and in different cultures, it was easy for me, as his tenant now, to feel goodwill in my heart for him. (*EA* 174–5)

Two, the writer's ability to observe and understand the present context is seen as the culmination of his growth. 'The Journey', a crucial central section of the narrative, is devoted to describing the various stages of self-realization through his efforts to become a writer and the different cultural exposures involved in these. The process of disappointment, reconciliations, and satisfaction which attended the writer's cultural and creative voyage from Trinidad to Salisbury is finally compressed in the symbolism of a surrealistic painting by Giorgio de Chirico, entitled *The Enigma of Arrival* by the poet Apollinaire. Three, the writer's empathetic understanding of the communal life and landscape of Salisbury (in which the writer symbolizes the healing effect, the 'rebirth', *EA* 157, that England had meant for him), gradually allows him to revisit and reconcile himself to his homeland, Trinidad. The final section of the book, 'The Ceremony of Farewells', describes his return to Trinidad to attend the cremation of a sister, and his involvement in the Hindu rituals attending this. He discovers there 'a sense of place' (as Naipaul has described it later), not dissimilar to the sense of place he apprehends in the decay and continuity of rural England:

> Our sacred world – the sanctities that had been handed down to us as children by our families, the sacred places of our childhood, sacred because we had seen them as children and had filled them with wonder, places doubly and trebly sacred to me because far away in England I had lived in them imaginatively over many books, and had in my fantasy set in those places the very beginning of things, had constructed out of them a fantasy of home, though I was to learn that the ground was bloody, that there had been aboriginal people there once, who had been killed or made to die away – our sacred world had vanished. Every generation was to take us further away from those sanctities. But we remade the world for ourselves; every generation does that, as we found when we came together for the death of this sister and felt the need to honour and remember. (*EA* 318)

In the course of readdressing so many of the themes and preoccupations of his earlier writings, and in concurrently re-examining his own engagement with the world, *The Enigma of Arrival* presents certain significant advances on Naipaul's prior views and attitudes. It may be observed that the distinctive features which emerge from this book provide an appropriate framework for any examination of his subsequent writings. The difference in the narrative strategies deployed in *The Enigma of Arrival* compared to earlier books is self-evident. *The Enigma of Arrival* is arguably Naipaul's most intimate book: there are no distanciation techniques involved (apart from the reminder of this being a novel) – on the contrary, the writer presents himself, his thoughts, and his world in the most unmediated fashion possible. The entire book is a meditation on the writer meditating on life, the world, and himself. It unravels with the fluidity and associational logic of a stream-of-consciousness novel. Moreover, while there are evocations of his earlier methods of cultural critique and evaluation, there is an overarching sense that the writer does not subscribe to these in quite the same manner. The counterpoint of mimic (colonized) and mimicked (colonizer) cultures surfaces at times, reminiscent of his denunciatory early writings on the Caribbean and Caribbean history on the one hand and on England (primarily *Mr Stone and the Knights Companions*) on the other, the play-acting and vacuousness of the former and the alienness/loneliness of the latter with its underlying affirmativeness. The violence of his writings on Africa and blackness is also evoked – especially when he speaks of his juxtaposition of African landscapes on a Wiltshire landscape in the act of writing *In a Free State*. But all these are now subsumed within an apprehension of something larger and more universal. As already observed, what preoccupies the writer here is the manner in which opposites and differences can ultimately be brought together. And Naipaul seems to suggest here that what allows all cultural and social differences and opposites to be brought together is a deeper spiritual desire which is manifested in the communal lives and cohesiveness of different societies, the manner in which people of different persuasions seek to accommodate themselves to their environments and each other, in the human ability to function within and in consonance with their histories and heritages, and in the human capacity for incremental readjustment when that is required.

Along with the more or less reconciliatory tendency of *The Enigma of Arrival* apropos the writer's engagement with the world, there is also an implicit ideological commitment. In the presentation of his views about human spiritual desires and needs, and the place of communal existence, environment and heritage therein, there emerges a primarily conservative[1] view of society. The idea appears to be that individuals and societies are not so much determining agents as subject to the larger determining movement of history itself. People and communities and cultures and societies are, in Naipaul's view, encapsulated by their basic spiritual needs and environments and heritages. Change is not, and cannot be, a voluntary and self-determined route, but something that emerges in a fraught fashion from the conflicts and clashes within the spiritual needs, environments and heritages of people. One can simply apprehend, Naipaul suggests, or become aware of communal spiritual and cultural truths, and the manner in which these impinge on the evolution of different cultures and societies; one cannot, it is to be inferred, hope to transcend these without falling into the vacuousness and superficiality which many of Naipaul's books deplore. What emerges in Naipaul's later writings, in other words, in not a transcendence of his earlier views and attitudes, but a bringing together of these in a basically conservative, and increasingly anti-revolutionary, understanding of human spirituality and society. This is, of course, far from explicit in *The Enigma of Arrival*, but it does become more explicit as he progresses from there. In *The Enigma of Arrival* itself, it is not insignificant that the clearest self-appraisal that Naipaul offers (as quoted above) is in relation to his aristocratic landlord.[2]

This ideological commitment is made clearer in *A Turn in the South*. The preoccupations of *A Turn in the South* are described as follows by Naipaul:

> My first travel book – undertaken at the suggestion of Eric Williams, the first black prime minister of Trinidad – had been about some of the former slave colonies of the Caribbean and South America. I was twenty eight then. It seemed to me fitting that my last travel book – travel on a theme – should be about the old slave states of the American Southeast.
>
> My thoughts – in Dallas, and then in New York, when I was planning the journey – were about the race issue. I didn't know then that that issue would quickly work itself out during the journey, and that my subject would become that other South – of order and faith, and music and melancholy – which I didn't know about, but of which I had been given an indication in Dallas. (*TS* 25)

The change in themes mentioned here is precisely what my earlier observations about the advances in Naipaul's perspective are about. Starting out with colonial history/culture and race (manifest in his cultural critiques of the Caribbean, and the focus of his attempt to write about blackness), and ending up with 'order and faith, and music and melancholy' (more consonant with *The Enigma of Arrival*), marks a process which *A Turn in the South* substantiates. There is a shift in priorities involved: the quotation suggests that the race issue was exhausted ('the issue would quickly work itself out'), and was either superseded or subsumed in the other issue (faith etc.). The interest of the book is largely in this shift of priorities (is the race issue superseded or subsumed? how and why?): this is what is new, so to say, about this stage of Naipaul's writings.

The book falls back on the by now familiar features of Naipaul's travel writing. It presents a series of interviews conducted by the writer (appearing to present 'documentary' evidence), with contextual details and minutiae thrown in (about the speech-patterns, appearances and circumstances of the interviewees, and about the landscape and environment they inhabit), and providing, of course, the writer's commentary as a kind of voice-over. It could be usefully thought of as the script of a documentary film. The interviewees that Naipaul chooses or comes across could be seen in terms of obvious categories: these include successful blacks (Hetty, ex-slave landowner; Al Murray, the Harlem writer; Hosea Williams, the high-profile civil liberties campaigner; a reputed woman Baptist pastor and social worker, Revd. Bernyce Clausell; academics from Booker T. Washington's Tuskegee University; and so on); Southern whites from former slave-owning backgrounds – some conservative (like Marion Sass and Jack Leland), some liberal (like Anne Siddons), some simply neutral; and later in the book a series of characters who could be thought of as experts by dint of their experiences, sensibilities or interests (about Southern history and local constitutions, about different religious communities, about country music and poetry, about rednecks).

What emerges from these series of interviews could be read as a continuous argument. Naipaul's initial explorations into the race issue persuades him that, despite continuing and effective social segregation regardless of official desegregation, the race issue is gradually on the way to becoming a non-issue. All the characteristic movements geared to redressing racial inequality – Martin Luther King style civil liberties activism, academic black studies – have been commodified and formalized through the media and rendered superficial and predictable. For the blacks this has meant either a meaningless adherence to dated protest gestures, or the acceptance of white middle-class values, or a sense of void. He doesn't revisit more radical black politics; presumably the views expressed in 'Michael X and the Black Power Killings in Trinidad' still hold. For the white conservatives this devolves in nostalgia and an attempt to come to terms with the 'irrationality' of a slave-owning past by evading the violence involved; for white liberals this has led to a floundering need for self-definition and understanding. What holds all the parties in question together is the desire to find some sort of spiritual satisfaction, usually expressed as a commitment to revealed religion. The encapsulation of faith, which increasingly becomes Naipaul's theme hereafter, is attested to by most of the interviewees – it is presented as the ubiquitous phenomenon of the southern American states. The persistence with which it is presented suggests that faith has an affirmative social role, and Naipaul uncharacteristically shows little desire to prick the surfaces of the spiritual discourses he encounters. Naipaul also unquestioningly presents some of the creative attempts to be quintessentially Southern (which deliberately expurgate the fraught race issue): Jim Applewhite's poetry, country music. And he dwells on, though more sceptically, the redneck lifestyle (who seek an uncomplicated natural existence, and 'definitely do not like blacks'). The assertion of faith, and the occasionally tainted attempts at reinventing Southernness, are all tinged with an air of pathos and soul-searching: but to Naipaul these have more of a final say about the South than any further exploration of racial inequality or any politics of social justice.

It is inevitably difficult to identify an ideological commitment which can be attributed to Naipaul here. The form of the book (presenting 'documentary' evidence) resists that. The South appears to be revealed (rather like the revealed religion some of his interviewees talk about) to Naipaul, rather than read or interpreted by him. Nevertheless, this apparent lack of ideological commitment is far from being consistent with *A Turn in the South*: the glibness with which activist black politics 'quickly works itself out', and the uncritical delineation of 'order and faith, and music and melancholy', are arguably indicative of such an ideological attitude. Naipaul's scepticism about political activism, and championing of awareness of heritage, incremental intellectual development and spiritual fulfilment – only discernible between the lines in *A Turn in the South* – are more clearly stated in *A Way in the World*.

A Way in the World is a collection of fictionalized and autobiographical pieces which address three areas: Naipaul's overrarching perception of Caribbean and post-colonial history; further autobiographical reflections in the light of his changing views; and intertwined with both of these are thoughts regarding idealistic or revolutionary politics. Two substantial sections of the book simply rewrite, with larger imaginative forays and fictionalizations, episodes and characters he had dealt with already in *The Loss of El Dorado*: the section entitled 'A Parcel of Papers, A Roll of Tobacco, a Tortoise' gives a close account of Sir Walter Raleigh's last days and of his relationship with an American Indian, Don José; and 'In the Gulf of Desolation' Naipaul details the Venezuelan revolutionary Francisco Miranda's final visit to the Caribbean and his correspondence at the time with his wife Sarah. Both accounts delineate similar patterns: Raleigh and Miranda are shown to be failed visionaries (Raleigh with his illusory quest for a rich and dazzling New World and Miranda with his quest for revolution) who are at odds with the realities that they encounter; and both accounts try to recreate the lost worlds that Raleigh and Miranda inhabited, which, despite their remoteness and transience, emphasize the essential and continuing triviality and banality of the colonial world and its societies. In both, the visionaries are motivated primarily by personal ambition, and are humanized through their personal relationships. The two extended sections present Naipaul's view of history and historical personalities. Naipaul's view of colonial history in *A Way in the World* is most conveniently outlined at two levels: one, colonial history is the record of remarkable changes (geological, demographic, cultural) with an underlying continuity (a banal and often brutal reality) – and this gradually works itself out in Naipaul's personal history and experiences; two, colonial history could be understood as the conflict of visionary or revolutionary ideas and the pettiness and brutality of colonial realities – this too is substantiated in Naipaul's lifetime, in his encounters with would-be modern revolutionaries. The book as a whole substantiates these two levels of Naipaul's view of the colonial past and present.

In *A Way in the World* a sense of transience stretches from the unrecorded and entirely erased pre-Colombian history which Naipaul considers briefly (*WW* 208–9), to the recorded phase of colonization which Naipaul dwells on in 'A Parcel of Papers, a Roll of Tobacco, a Tortoise' and 'In the Gulf of Desolation', to the disappearing world of Naipaul's own childhood and youth (especially delineated in the autobiographical section entitled 'History: A Smell of Fish Glue'), to the wider colonial world that Naipaul encounters in his travels (particularly in his Venezuelan travels, as described in the section 'A New Man'). Paradoxically, this sense of transience which emanates from the fact of change also becomes a conceptual constant. The faint melancholy of transience, the instability of change, and the air of disappointment which attends the inevitability of change, pervade all of history as Naipaul portrays it. All human existence within the ebb and flow of colonial history has an appropriate sense of being determined from outside; and all human endeavour in colonial contexts is dwarfed and rendered trite by the largeness of historical changes and their inevitability. No notion of political agency (a colonial or anti-colonial effort) is allowed to insert itself effectively in Naipaul's view of colonial history: Naipaul's colonial history – from pre-history to personal history – merely shows the encapsulation of humanity within the indifference and brutality of historical change. It is this sameness of scope which becomes the index of continuity in Naipaul's view of colonial history.

Within this view of history, carefully cultivated over a range of anecdotal and fictional narratives, are placed the personalities who try to be determinative agents, who bring change. In colonial history this is the colonizer (Raleigh here) and the revolutionary (Miranda), both of whom, despite their fixity of purpose and determination, are made subject to and defeated by the process of history. The reality of their times defeats them, and that reality is the reality of the world in its historical continuum. There is continuity too in the failure of idealistic and visionary human efforts: as in Raleigh and Miranda in the past, it is seen to recur in characters within the author's times – characters like Foster Morris (the section entitled 'Passenger: A Figure from the Thirties' is devoted to him) and Lebrun (who figures largely in the section 'On the Run').

63

Foster Morris wrote the first politically sympathetic and apparently balanced account of the oil-field workers' strike in Trinidad under Uriah Butler, *The Shadowed Livery* (1937). In the course of a series of encounters with him in London in the fifties, Naipaul realizes that the entire politically motivated account in *The Shadowed Livery* had been a lie: Foster Morris had carefully concealed the debilitating racial fractures and conflicts which were wedded to the oil-workers' strike. When Naipaul digs deeper into Foster Morris's character, he finds a person who is himself defeated by the banality and inevitability of the real world (where people, including himself, simply *are* racially motivated and work within small vested interests). And Naipaul implies that this is not simply the unique experience of Foster Morris, it is symptomatic of the entire ethos of political and social optimism which engendered him. Foster Morris is, as Naipaul carefully makes out, 'A Figure from the Thirties', associated with all the well-known British writers of the thirties. The thirties were, of course, the decade of great political expectations, optimism, and conflict – polarized between revolutionary socialism and fascism. Similarly, in Lebrun, a flamboyant Marxist revolutionary who was associated with the oil-workers' strike and the black civil rights movement, who (the narrator declares) had considerable intellectual gifts and powers of expression, and who had (as the narrator discovers) an impressive international following, Naipaul finds another lie and failure. His chequered career is followed by Naipaul to the end, which happens in an African country where Lebrun is found advocating racial and cultural purity. Naipaul's most promising revolutionaries and visionaries are not only failures before the vast canvas of history, they are also failures in a theoretical sense. In their psyche radical socialism and fascism seem paradoxically to gravitate towards each other. As in Morris, in Lebrun also Naipaul perceives a larger phenomenon – Lebrun represents the history of blackness as Naipaul saw it exemplified in Africa and Africans (I have discussed this already).

Clearly, Naipaul's later writings show a more focused preoccupation with historical determinism and spiritual needs. These are arguably bound by a consistently conservative ideological position: one in which history has to be apprehended, but in which history cannot be humanly determined; in which people who try to perform their functions in society in a self-aware fashion are sympathetically viewed, and those who try to change society are seen as dogmatic and dangerous and destructive; in which those who come to terms with their heritage have hope, and those who wish to overturn their heritage are deluded; in which faith can be healing and rationalism can be false and lacerating; in which spiritual satisfaction comes from a sense of being at one with heritage and place, and spiritual dissatisfaction attends any dislocation and disregard for heritage. In many ways, this is no more than a continuation of Naipaul's black-and-white mode of looking at things. However, the issues of spiritual necessity and faith present further complexities within the conservative scheme outlined here: to examine these I turn to Naipaul's exploration of Islam and Islamic countries.

7

Writing About Islam

The complexity of Naipaul's engagement with the issues which appear in his mature writings – the spiritual requirements of people, cultural heritage and historical determinism, and faith – is probably best gauged in his two books about Islamic countries and Islam: *Among the Believers: An Islamic Journey* (1981) and *Beyond Belief: Islamic Excursions Among the Converted Peoples* (1998). Both are travel books: clearly, despite asseverations to the contrary in *A Turn in the South*, that was not to be his last travel book. *Among the Believers* presents Naipaul's observations on Islam, Islamic states and Muslims in the course of travels in Iran, Pakistan, Malaysia and Indonesia in 1979; and *Beyond Belief* is a follow-up on *Among the Believers*, in which he describes his visits to the same countries sixteen years later. The two books together clarify some of Naipaul's thoughts on issues that held his interest. The clarification works at two levels. In the course of putting together details about his encounters with and thoughts about Islam he comes up with a perspective specifically on Islam, but he also manages to make points of general social, cultural and historical import. The two levels of clarification are concretized in the development between the two books (or between experiences which are separated by sixteen years). *Among the Believers* has an exploratory air about it: it comes to its subject matter with an assumption of ignorance, and the process of putting together and thinking about observations as they occur forms the substance of the book – though these are, tacitly, dependent on modes of cultural evaluation Naipaul had developed already. *Beyond Belief* has, naturally, an air of retrospection about it: it is more statemental in approach, and presents a concretized and confirmed thesis about Islam itself and about the general issues in question.

Among the Believers ostensibly sets out with a specific question: in what way do Muslims expect Islam to facilitate the creation of an ideal Islamic state, and what sort of concrete shape (in economic, technological and political terms) is the latter likely to take? This is the question which Naipaul repeatedly puts to those he meets in the four countries he visits, and he tries to meet those who are likely to be able to provide an answer. He also tries to present the perspective of those who have unwittingly or passively become the subjects of such an enterprise: ordinary citizens who find themselves in the process or outcome of attempts to realize an Islamic state. The question which Naipaul takes with him on his travels in Islamic countries is appropriate to the context in which he makes his journey. Iran had just experienced the throes of an Islamic revolution and the autocracy of the Shah had been replaced by a theocracy led by the Islamic clerisy under Ayatollah Khomeini. Pakistan, barely four decades after partition from India, had moved from democracy under Zulfikar Ali Bhutto to the military dictatorship of General Zia ul Haq, and a hardening of its theocratic constitution. Indonesia and Malaysia had also seen massive upheavals in an era of post-colonization and were then witnessing the rise of significant pan-Islamic or 'fundamentalist' political forces. Naipaul's explorations of these contexts and issues are not, however, systematic examinations of either. The books are, as he says, primarily a collection of 'stories' or narratives about those whom he meets, often in their own words. The personal backgrounds and perspectives of the people he meets are inextricably mixed up with the social and political issues and contexts which are examined.

The points Naipaul makes about the Islamic polity and about the personal dimension of those subject to it in Among the Believers could be summarized as follows.

(1) Islam is, Naipaul suggests, a dogmatic set of rules which were created to be consonant with the spiritual, social and imperial aspirations of the medieval Arabia of and after the Prophet. Islamic dogma emanates in an authoritarian rather than a rational fashion: it devolves ultimately from the authority of the Prophet and, through him, the Koran (directly from Allah), and more immediately from the authority of Islamic leaders (usually from within the clerisy). The cornerstone of Islam, therefore, is

not social and political efficaciousness but absolute unquestioning faith in the dogma and its authorities. The authority and the dogma in its unbending form is all that matters, Naipaul observes, irrespective of the context in which the faith manifests itself. Islam is therefore indifferent to the changes of history, or reads history only as a confirmation of its truth.

(2) Since Islamic dogma is impervious to the dictates of social and political changes it has maintained even in the modern world its medieval regressive character. Naipaul repeatedly reminds his readers of the regressive nature of Islamic dogma as it is applied in the Islamic organizations he visits: in the appalling situation of women, in the medieval techniques of acquiring Islamic learning (through rote), in the brutality of its legal procedures, in authoritarian and anachronistic modes of social control that can be observed at all levels.

(3) Though Islamic dogma and authority refused any accommodation with change, and are seen by their proponents as an alternative to the technologically and politically evolved societies of the West, they are in fact dependant on that non-Islamic (especially Western) world. Proponents of Islamic states do accept the technological and scientific know-how and imports of the West, and use these to promote Islam in the modern world. Naipaul cites various instances of the use of Western technology, and more insidiously of Western rationalistic terminology (fragments of socialist theory, bits of Ivan Illich's theory of education,[1] etc.), by proponents of Islam – reminiscent of the notion of mimicry Naipaul had used earlier.

(4) The fixed medieval quality of Islamic dogma and its paradoxical readiness to accept what can be got from non-Islamic societies means that no concrete and realizable Islamic state can actually be conceived and attained (despite ambitions thereof, and actual Islamic revolutions). Naipaul observes ironically that:

> the Islamic enterprise was enormous: it was the deliberate creation – with only the Koran as a guide – of a state mechanism that would function in the modern world and would be unlike anything else that had evolved. It was a high intellectual enterprise. (AB 112),

and eventually concludes:

This late twentieth-century Islam appeared to raise political issues. But it had the flaw of its origins – the flaw that ran through Islamic history: to the political issues it raised it offered no political or practical solution. It offered only the faith. It offered only the Prophet, who would settle everything – but who had ceased to exist. This political Islam was rage, anarchy. (*AB* 331)

(5) It follows therefore that proponents of Islamic dogma are not a creative force. They do not actually have any clear and practicable Islamic state to work towards; their only agenda is to dominate what has already been created without it and to impose the faith. Naipaul sees this in every aspect of Islamic symbology; for example, even in the symbolic connotations of the veils that some Malay village women wear in Kuala Lumpur:

> The veil is more than the veil; it is a mask of aggression. Not like the matted locks of the Ras Tafarian in Jamaica, a man dulled by a marginal life that has endured for generations; not like the gear of the middle-class hippie, who wishes only to drop out; these are the clothes of uprooted village people who wish to pull down what is not theirs and then take over. Because an unacknowledged part of the fantasy is that the world goes on, runs itself, has only to be inherited. (*AB* 216)

There are some ancillary points which need to be made to convey what Naipaul does in *Among the Believers*. Naipaul recognizes, and is often impressed by, the force of Islamic faith on individuals and by the role this has played on individual backgrounds and aspirations. His portrayal of individuals is often sympathetic. Naipaul is struck, for instance, by the Malaysian Shafi's openness, sincere Islamic passion, and nostalgic vision of a simplified Malay rural community – and Shafi is far from being the only proponent of Islam who is rendered in this sympathetic fashion. Naipaul sees individual Muslims with Islamic ideals or those who are subject to Islamic organizations as trapped by their religion. Naipaul suggests that individuals, whether active proponents of Islamic dogma and ideals or passively subject to these, are enclosed by the unbending form of Islamic faith and its constraints. Individuals are determined by the spirit of Islam and are unable to determine themselves in creative or progressive ways on that account. A significant aspect of Naipaul's view of Islamic countries and their peoples is, therefore, that rage and anxiety and dissatisfaction and impotence (usually expressed through Islam rather than against Islam) subsume them. To put it simplistically in the light of Naipaul's preoccupation with the spiritual needs of people and the issue of faith noted in his other writings: *Among the Believers* asserts that Islamic faith and dogma are designed to impoverish the spiritual needs and growth of its practitioners, whether they realize it or not.

Finally, it is also worth noting that *Among the Believers* draws a constant parallel (in keeping with the mature Naipaul's anti-revolutionary and conservative ideology) between revolutionary socialist idealism and dogmatic Islamic ideals. He presents characters (his guide, Behzad, and Behzad's girlfriend, in Iran, for example) whose revolutionary fervour is as dogmatic and arbitrary and unrealistic as the Islamic revolutions and pan-Islamic movements which have overtaken them. Naipaul observes that socialist revolutionary sentiments in Islamic contexts tend to be simply a reactive black-and-white opposition, lacking in a rational basis as well. It is suggested between the lines that in their forms and in the scale of social violence there is little to differentiate a socialist revolution and an Islamic revolution. And he often finds himself encountering simplified versions of socialist terminology and analysis in the words of proponents of Islamic revolution. He finds this akinness of socialist revolution and Islamic revolution in the development of Indonesian politics – from Sukarno's socialist idealism to Suharto's gradual acquiring of Islamic faith, and Habibie's technocratic Islamic vision. In *Among the Believers*, a chapter entitled 'The Interchangeable Revolutions' makes the point clearly:

> *To replace all this.* Islam sanctified rage – rage about the faith, political rage; one could be like the other. And more than once on this journey I had met sensitive men who were ready to contemplate great convulsions.
>
> In Iran there had been Behzad, who had shown me Tehran and the holy cities of Qom and the Mashhad. He was the communist son of a communist father, not a Muslim. But his communism was like a version of the Shia faith of Iran, a version of the Shia rage about injustice: a rage rooted in the overthrow by the Arabs of the old Persian empire in the seventh century. Good Muslims believed that the best time in the world was the time of the Prophet and the first

four good caliphs; Behzad believed that the best time was in Russia between 1917 and 1953. [. . .] Ayatollah Khomeini spoke in the name of God the avenger; Behzad, the communist, spoke like Khomeini. (*AB* 354)

Beyond Belief (1998), which describes Naipaul's visit to the same four countries again sixteen years later (1995), reiterates for the larger part the same observations. The difference from *Among the Believers* is, as I have said, that the earlier book has more of an exploratory air about it while the latter is more statemental. Naipaul finds that the sixteen intervening years have largely confirmed his observations about the Islamic polity and its subjects: he finds confirmation of the regressive nature of Islamic dogma in all the countries he revisits. Where *Among the Believers* had concluded that Islamic dogma and faith, with their authoritarian proponents, have no concrete and realizable state to look forward to (are, on the contrary, backward-looking), and simply expect to dominate (and are dependent on) cultures that are not inherently Islamic, *Beyond Belief* begins with the more hard-nosed assertion that Islamic expansion outside Arabia is no more than the most debilitating form of imperialism. The tone is set in the Prologue:

Islam is in its origins an Arab religion. Everyone not an Arab who is a Muslim is a convert. Islam is not simply a matter of conscience or private belief. It makes imperial demands. A convert's world view alters. His holy places are in Arab lands; his sacred language is Arabic. His idea of history alters. He rejects his own; he becomes, whether he likes it or not, a part of the Arab story. The convert has to turn away from everything that is his. The disturbance for societies is immense, and even after a thousand years can remain unresolved; the turning away has to be done again and again. People develop fantasies about who and what they are; and in the Islam of converted countries there is an element of neurosis and nihilism. These countries can be easily set on the boil. (*BB* 1)

These sentiments are not inconsistent with the observations of *Among the Believers*; and yet, in being given the air of a conclusive statement, they acquire previously unremarked nuances. Naipaul's perspective on Islam becomes in this statement more consistent with his examination of colonizer–colonized cultural relationships. The vast phenomenon of Islamic expansion (vast both in terms of time and territory) is more explicitly analysed in terms of the mimicked–mimic counterpoint that was available in his early writings on the Caribbean and on India. Islam anywhere outside the Arab lands becomes automatically denunciatable in the dismissive tone with which Naipaul had surveyed the colonial and post-colonial culture of the Caribbean and India. Indeed, it is worse – because, in Naipaul's view, Islamic imperialism is regressive and medieval, whereas there is something liberal and positive about the imperial West. In Naipaul's opinion Western imperialism allowed for 'intellectual' development and the growth of a sense of history, whereas Islamic imperialism has simply impoverished 'intellectual' growth. For him this is exemplified in the comparative experiences of India and Pakistan:

> The British period [in India] – two hundred years in some places, less than a hundred in others – was a time of Hindu regeneration. The Hindus, especially in Bengal, welcomed the New Learning of Europe and the institutions the British brought. The Muslims, wounded by their loss of power, and out of old religious scruples, stood aside. It was the beginning of the intellectual distance between the two communities. This distance has grown with independence; and it is this – more even than religion now – that at the end of the twentieth century has made India and Pakistan quite distinct countries. India, with an intelligentsia that grows by leaps and bounds, expands in all directions. Pakistan, proclaiming only the faith and then proclaiming the faith again, ever shrinks. (BB 65)

Of Naipaul's view of India, and especially of Naipaul's view of India as Hindu, I have more to say in the next chapter. For the moment it is worth noting that Naipaul in *Beyond Belief* brings his perspective on Islam closer to his earlier modes of cultural evaluation.

There are further nuances in that preliminary quotation from the Prologue. There reappears an implicit notion of authentic cultures: of something that is indelibly the 'converted' people's *own*, their *own* dispossessed 'holy lands', their *own* 'sacred languages'. This is probably best described as a kind of cultural essentialism; the notion of a heritage that underlies all external domination and convulsion, that remains unassimilated and self-contained over thousands of years, that is suppressed by the Islamic phenomenon and waits to be revitalized in some period of 'intellectual' regeneration (as it was for the Hindus, with the aid of a 'liberal' British period). Cultural essentialism had also appeared significantly in Naipaul's earlier writings. It has been examined above in the context of Naipaul's attempts to write about blackness and Black Power – though in that context it was a primeval, violent, racial thing. *Beyond Belief* is littered with sympathetic encounters with authentic and essential cultural manifestations. This has surprised some of the reviewers of *Beyond Belief*[2] but there is nothing unexpected about it. It is the logical outcome of Naipaul's world view. Unsurprisingly one comes across avowals of sympathy for mystical pre-Islamic cultural manifestations in *Beyond Belief*:

> Perhaps it is this absence of the sense of sacredness – which is more than the idea of the 'environment' – that is the curse of the New World, and is the curse especially of Argentina and ravaged places like Brazil. And perhaps it is this sense of sacredness – rather than history and the past – that we of the New World travel to the old to rediscover.
>
> So it is strange to someone of my background that in the converted Muslim countries – Iran, Pakistan, Indonesia – the fundamentalist rage is against the past, against history, and the impossible dream is of the true faith growing out of a spiritual vacancy. (*BB* 59)

This sympathy extends to the Indonesian Dewi Fortuna Anwar's animistic pre-Islamic sentiments, and resurfaces when he visits Pasargadae's pre-Islamic Zoroastrian temple and Cyrus's palace in Iran, and again when he describes the life of the *bomoh* in Malaysia.

Along with the analysis of Islamic expansion as a particularly damaging imperial phenomenon, and the reappearance of an explicit cultural essentialism, *Beyond Belief* simply reiterates the observations of *Among the Believers*. But there is that difference in tone: in the earlier book the observations had been searching, in the later book they appear with more conviction. The sense of cultural depletion due to the domination of Islam is made stronger, expressed with more bitterness, and offered as a confirmation of Naipaul's particular perspective on Islam. In *Beyond Belief* Naipaul revisits places he had been to before and tries to revisit the people he had met earlier. Indonesia had obviously prospered in the sixteen intervening years, as had the dissident Islamic leader and lecturer Imaduddin whom he had met before. Imaduddin had become an important government person in the interim, close to Habibie and Habibie's vision of a technocratic Islamic revival, and pioneer of the Association of Muslim Intellectuals. Naipaul sees in this success story little more than a threat to the essential pre-Islamic cultural forms:

> In Indonesia we were almost at the limit of the Islamic world. For a thousand years or so until 1400 this had been a cultural and religious part of Greater India: animist, Buddhist, Hindu. Islam had come here not long before Europe. It had not been the towering force it had been in other converted places. For the last two hundred years, in a colonial world, Islam had been on the defensive, the religion of a subject people. It had not completely possessed the souls of people. It was still a missionary religion. It had been kept alive informally in colonial times, in simple village boarding schools, descended perhaps as an idea from Buddhist monasteries.
>
> To possess or control these schools was to possess power. And I began to feel that Imaduddin and the Association of Muslim Intellectuals – with their stress on science and technology, and their dismissing of old ritual ways – aimed at nothing less. The ambition was stupendous: to complete the take-over of this part of the world, and to take the islands to their destiny as the leader of Islamic revival in the twenty-first century. (*BB* 24)

Other success stories of Indonesian Muslims are presented: Lukman Umar, the publisher; Budi, the computer software designer. Lukman Umar's enterprise is seen to prey on the vacuum of Muslim students' and women's intellectual lives, and he finally goes into labour-export; and Budi's Islamic faith hides his deep-seated loneliness. These are countered by the nostalgic reflections of a pastoral idyll animated by pre-Islamic spirits in Dewi Fortuna Anwar's family traditions and the Javanese Linus's poetry (the latter under threat from local Muslims).

As Naipaul moves away from the outer limits of the Islamic world, where Islam is still growing and ambitious and there is evident prosperity, and moves into the heartland of the converted Islamic world, the picture grows grimmer. In the sixteen years since his previous visit both Pakistan and Iran have been, Naipaul observes, devastated by war, by the effects of regressive Islamic dogmatism, by internecine conflict, and by the spiritual dissatisfaction of the people. Violence and bitterness subsume both countries as Naipaul sees them, and he focuses on them and describes them with an air of confirming his suspicions about the Islamic polity and its future, and his reading of the nature of Islam. Description on description of people despairing in different ways, or being drawn to violence, or being crushed by violence, make *Beyond Belief* a far darker affair than *Among the Believers* – *Beyond Belief* is written, one feels, to document against Islam, not to explore it, as in the earlier book. Documentation is what Naipaul wants to be seen to be doing here. In the Prologue he characteristically effaces himself and suggests that the 'stories' speak for themselves (a ploy he had used more disingenuously in *The Loss of El Dorado*):

> It is less of a travel book; the writer is less present, less of an inquirer. He is in the background, trusting to his instinct, a discoverer of people, a finder-out of stories. These stories, opening out one from the other, *make their own pattern and define each country and its promptings*; and the four sections of the book make a whole. (*BB* 2; my emphasis)

So 'stories' pile up as evidence against Islam and for Naipaul's view of Islam: stories of the experience of soldiers in the Iran–Iraq war, in the Baluchi resistance to the Pakistani army, in feudal conflict in frontier towns in Pakistan; stories of ordinary people who are victimized by the Islamic state (the entrepreneur Ali, the journalist Jaffrey, the guide Mehrdad, etc.); stories about the terrible oppression of women (most memorably in the story of the Nawab of Bhawalpur); and so on. But this vast collection of 'stories' would have no intrinsic shape without Naipaul's all-comprehending concept of Islam as a regressive imperialist phenomenon, and without his cultural essentialist thinking. The documentary evidence is there, but it all makes only a particular kind of sense and seems relevant in a particular fashion because Naipaul has set it out in his given framework. The 'stories' do not strictly speak for themselves, and Naipaul's observations are not actually simply corollary to the stories, the end of an inductive process. The stories fit into Naipaul's elucidated perspective.

And, in keeping with Naipaul's consistently anti-revolutionary and anti-socialist ideology, there are also stories of failed and deluded socialist revolutionaries: the entrepreneur Ali's frightening encounter with revolutionary political prisoners; the despair of the ex-revolutionary Paydar; the sham of the unrepentant revolutionary Shahbaz's contribution to the Baluchi resistance (here Naipaul is far from invisible, he provides a constant and sarcastic voice-over).

So, Naipaul's two books about Islam provide a clear sense of the direction which he ideologically moves towards in his mature preoccupations. He brings his black-and-white colonial mind with its understanding of mimic and mimicked cultures, and he brings his mature reflections on the spiritual needs of the people, the nature of faith and historical determination, to the new (for him) area of Islam. An analysis of Islam is conducted in *Among the Believers* – in the searching manner of a person who is ignorant of its nuances, unacquainted with the languages of the people he speaks to, who wishes to record and assess only what he sees and hears. From these he reaches certain damning conclusions about the political aspirations and dogmatism and authoritarianism of proponents of Islam in the modern world. *Beyond Belief* follows up these observations after a sixteen-year interval, and for the most part finds his analysis and expectations confirmed. He brings his analysis of Islam more in line with the modes of cultural evaluation he had evolved in other social, usually colonial/post-colonial, contexts. More interestingly, he reveals more explicitly than heretofore a sympathy for 'authentic' cultures and heritages, which can be appropriately described in this context as a form of cultural essentialism.

Naipaul's readers may feel justifiably sceptical of Naipaul's approach to and analysis of Islam, even while recognizing the veracity of the situations he describes. It may be argued that the generalizations that Naipaul makes are based on flimsy and insubstantial ground: sheer observation and documentation of 'stories' do not necessarily permit the kind of general insights into the theology, history, politics and sociology of Islam that he offers. The term Islam is not rigorously defined: Naipaul uses it to describe a medley of phenomena, the links between which are assumed rather than given. Arguably, to be able to offer the kind of generalizations that Naipaul aspires to a much sounder background in Islamic theology and history is required, and in sociological and political theory. It might also be justifiably maintained that Naipaul does not so much understand Islam as accommodate it to his own pre-assumed conservative and anti-revolutionary ideology. That Naipaul seems unable to discern between socialist and Islamic revolutions suggests a superficial understanding of the former – and his reflections on both are largely guided by superficial comments about social psyche ('fantasies' are mentioned rather a lot) and verbal forms of communication (across an obvious language barrier).

Such scepticism would be matter for debate amongst those who are engaged in the analysis and understanding of the many-sided meanings and applications and effects of Islam in the modern world. On a somewhat different note, some of Naipaul's readers may also feel worried about the precise political implications of the position he increasingly clearly begins to espouse: the position which becomes conditional not only to his anti-revolutionary and conservative thinking, but more controversially to his notions of 'authentic' cultures, spiritual needs, heritage – in short, to his cultural essentialism. The precise political implications are more easily charted with regard to his writings on India, to which I now turn in the final chapter.

8

Writing About India, and Conclusion

I have kept the discussion of Naipaul's writings about India for the end precisely because these provide a useful overview of Naipaul's development as a whole (appropriate to a conclusion). Through these I can rehearse all the stages in the development of the Naipaul *œuvre* that have been charted above, and the more recent of these give interesting insights into Naipaul's political and ideological commitments now. Naipaul's excavations into Caribbean history were initiated in terms of personal history (the Indian indentured labourer ancestry, the childhood within an insular Hindu Trinidad community), and naturally throughout his writing career he has determinedly tried to understand India. The interest which began with regard to a largely unknown and mythical space in his personal history ('an area of darkness'), and gradually concretized itself in subsequent visits and revisits, through an expanding range of encounters, through disappointments and reanalyses, is indubitably a significant preoccupation across his career. At any rate, his writings about (and visits to) India are spread evenly over four decades: these include *An Area of Darkness* (1964); essays about India which appear in *The Overcrowded Barracoon* (1972); *India: A Wounded Civilization* (1977); *India: A Million Mutinies Now* (1990); and a series of short articles and interviews in various papers and magazines since 1990. Naipaul has revisited India as recently as early 1998.

Written in the early 1960s, *An Area of Darkness* delineates the author's first visit to and engagement with India in terms of the modes of cultural analysis he had developed already. Naipaul had, by this time, sorted out his view of the New World:

fictionalized reminiscences of the Hindu Trinidad of his childhood, speculations on his encounter with England and Englishness, and exploration of a range of Caribbean and South American countries had thrown up for him a consistent idea of the New World. Naipaul felt persuaded that the New World was caught up in a cultural vacuum; that it was bound to a fantasy play-acting which denies itself; that the West – the former colonizers and neo-colonists – provided images and aspirations which were constantly mimicked in the New World. The New World, in short, is a mimic culture, and the West is mimicked. It is this critical apparatus that Naipaul brings with him in his first encounter with India. In *An Area of Darkness* Naipaul finds evidence of play-acting and mimicry pretty much everywhere in India too: in the complex bureaucratic procedures which overtake the writer in search of a liquor licence; in the westernized business executives (with nicknames like Bunty, Andy, Freddy, Jimmy, etc.) and their lifestyles; in the bourgeois Mrs Mahindra in Delhi who confesses, 'I am craze for foreign, just craze for foreign'; in the manner in which he is treated and the relationships he forms with people during a longish sojourn in Kashmir; in the alienated and lonely and occasionally violent Sikh he meets in the train.

But in *An Area of Darkness* Naipaul is also struck from the beginning by the difference from the kind of mimicry he had encountered in Trinidad and the New World generally:

> The outer and inner worlds do not have the physical separateness which they had for us in Trinidad. They coexist; the [Indian] society only pretends to be colonial; and for this reason its absurdities are at once apparent. Its mimicry is both less and more than a colonial mimicry. It is the special mimicry of an old country which has been without a native aristocracy for a thousand years and has learned to make room for outsiders, but only at the top. The mimicry changes, the inner world remains constant: this is the secret of survival. [...] Yesterday the mimicry was Moghul; tomorrow it might be Russian or American; today it is English. (*AD* 56)

The difference is the difference between the aftermath of colonization in the old world and the New World. According to Naipaul, in India mimicry is a purely nihilistic phenomenon – it tries to negate something that is essentially Indian, that is linked to a pre-colonial period (and colonialism in India, according to

Naipaul, goes back a thousand years). The mimicry has more of an air of artificiality about it because even as it tries to supersede that essentially Indian past, it in fact fails: the essential Indian quality survives at the bottom ('outsiders' at the top), enclosed in an 'inner world [that] remains constant'. So the Indian colonial mimicry is somehow more false, a twice-removed mimicry, a make-belief which stretches across the tendentious attempt at negating what is indelibly Indian in favour of that which is inappropriately English. It is twice removed: not merely a mimicking of the West, but a mimicking of colonialism itself. The New World on the other hand is seen by Naipaul to be more comfortably *colonial*: its mimicry is only at one remove, it simply mimics the West. It is this uncomplicated vacuousness behind the make-belief which makes the New World simply and innocently colonial. When Naipaul compares Trinidad to India in the latter part of the book, Trinidad appears in a comparatively simple and happy light:

> Colonial India I could not link with colonial Trinidad. Trinidad was a British colony; but every child knew that we were only a dot on the map of the world, and it was therefore important to be British: that at least anchored us within a wider system. It was a system which we did not find oppressive; and though British, in institutions and education as well as in political fact, we were in the New World, our population was greatly mixed, English people were few and kept themselves to themselves, and England was as a result only one of the countries of which we were aware. (*AD* 188)

This difference is a running motif in the book, and *An Area of Darkness* is largely about that. This doesn't mean that Naipaul sets out in the book to discern what that essential and indelible Indian quality consists in – that, predictably and significantly, came later. In *An Area of Darkness* he is concerned primarily with describing the nuances of the unique kind of colonial mimicry he found in India, and with charting its (largely adverse) effects. That is the importance of this book: in his first encounter with India Naipaul doesn't try to delve into its essentially Indian depths, he is content to examine its peculiar old world variety of colonial mimicry and to observe the effects. The exercise is no more than an Indian version of *The Middle Passage*. The difference in the quality of the mimicry is examined at length in the chapter entitled 'Fantasy and Ruins'. Here Naipaul outlines nuances of Englishness, inferred largely from literary works in English set in India (the unavoidable Kipling and Forster). His sentiments about the impact of England on India (the mimicked manifestations) are probably most pointedly made there in his observations on architecture. He cites two kinds of colonial architecture, and his observations on these speak for themselves. He notes that the typically English architecture in India (Fort St George in Madras, Clive's House in Calcutta) is simply an 'incongruous imposition' – 'This is one aspect of Indian England; it belonged to the history of India; it was dead' (AD 190). The more hybridized and alive architecture of the Raj (which, he observes, is distinct from the typically English architecture) also makes a negative impression:

> With one part of myself I felt the coming together of England and India as a violation; with the other I saw it as ridiculous, resulting in a comic mixture of costumes and the widespread use of an imperfectly understood language. But there was something else, something at which the architecture of the Raj hinted: those collectorates, in whose vaults lay the fruits of an immense endeavour, those clubs, those circuit houses, those inspection houses, those first-class railway waiting rooms. Their grounds were a little too spacious; their ceilings a little too high, their columns and arches and pediments a little too rhetorical; they were neither of England nor India; they were a little too grand for their purpose, too grand for the puniness, poverty and defeat in which they were set. (AD 190–1)

These observations on English-Indian architecture could be taken as symptomatic of the old world's accommodation of colonialism, its twice removed mimicry, in general. The idea is that, however one looks at it, the English impact on India and India's reception of it is uncreative and retrogressive (a view that Naipaul was to modify later in comparison to Islamic 'imperialism') – it is either dead, or incongruous and self-defeating. Naipaul characteristically does not think much of the potential for hybridization: the Raj architecture merely under-lines the sense of defeat in India; the mixture of costumes is simply ridiculous; the Indian's attempt to adopt the English language is always perverse and 'imperfectly understood'.

The larger part of *An Area of Darkness* falls into place once one grasps Naipaul's appraisal of the twice removed old world mimicry of colonial/post-colonial India. The sensitivity to visions

81

of disease and decrepitude, which take on an almost symbolic quality in Naipaul's view, make sense: they are visible manifestations of the sense of defeat which pervades post-colonial India. The inability of Indians to understand their Indianness as a whole, their penchant for seeing themselves in the smallest regional or communal alignments, is a part of the defeat of the old world. Naipaul devotes some interesting passages to analysing the nation-building role of Gandhi and Nehru: both of whom, he asserts, had acquired their sense of the wholeness of India by dint of an exposure to the outer world, by cultivating an exterior perspective. Naipaul reiterates the notion of a lack of historical sense amongst Indians (a commonplace in early Western historiographical thinking, to be found in Hegel, Marx, Spengler, Toynbee and others) as another effect of his sense of defeat:

> It is well that Indians are unable to look at their country directly, for the distress they would see would drive them mad. And it is well that they have no sense of history, for how would they be able to squat amid their ruins, and which Indian would be able to read the history of his country for the last thousand years without anger and pain? It is better to retreat into fantasy and fatalism [...] (*AD* 201)

With these sentiments Naipaul proceeds to (literally and cruelly) dissociate himself from his family connections in India, and concludes with a feeling of relief at having enjoyed a colonial Trinidadian past, and a sense of comfort (rather like Forster's character Fielding in *A Passage to India*) in finding a place within the order of Europe.

An Area of Darkness is however an incomplete book. It does, as I have observed above, analyse what Naipaul sees as the twice removed old world mimicry of India and its effects. But implied in that argument is the notion of an essential old world India which, though defeated and self-negating, underlies all that mimicry; which survives despite, and perhaps because of, its experiences of colonization. *An Area of Darkness* gestures towards this alleged essential India often but does not describe it in a coherent fashion. Clearly, after writing *An Area of Darkness* Naipaul felt a need to go into this at greater length. By 1967 he begins to find in India a need to turn to something that is not mimicry; and though he doesn't state this explicitly it may be inferred that this need could be answered by an apprehension of the allegedly essential India. In an essay entitled 'A Second Visit' (*Daily Telegraph Magazine*, 11–18 August 1967) he states:

> Every discipline, skill and proclaimed ideal of the modern Indian state is a copy of something which is known to exist in its true form somewhere else. The student of cabinet government looks to Westminster as to the answers at the back of a book. The journals of protest look, even for their typography, to the *New Statesman*. So Indians, the holy men included, have continually to look outside India for approval. Fragmentation and dependence are complete. Local judgement is valueless. It is even as if, without the foreign chit, Indians can have no confirmation of their own reality.
>
> But India, though not a country, is unique. To its problems imported ideas no longer answer. The result is frenzy. (OB 94)

Arguably, it is with a view to dealing with the notion of an essential India that Naipaul wrote *India: A Wounded Civilization*.

The agenda of *India: A Wounded Civilization* (1977) – that is to say, exploring the essential India underlying the mimicry – falls in neatly with Naipaul's broader cultural essentialist thinking of the seventies. He already had his formulations about the Black Power movement and *Guerrillas* behind him; his thoughts about Africa were clear to him (*In a Free State* was already published, and *A Bend in the River* was to appear a couple of years later); and *A Wounded Civilization* was probably the formative point of the presumptions he took with him when he set off to explore Islamic countries in 1979. The thesis of *A Wounded Civilization* is twofold: that the essential India, the old world India, is purely Hindu and that a typically Hindu psyche and Hindu attitudes to life are pervasive in modern India; and that the integral and purely Hindu India was conquered and dominated first by Islam and later by the British, which has resulted in a stultification of the intellectual development and creativity of the essentially Hindu India. There is a sort of sub-thesis attached to these: that the longer period of Islamic domination (finally established with the fall of the Hindu kingdom of Vijaynagar in 1565, he says) has been particularly retrogressive and damaging for an essentially Hindu India (in this he looks forward to his books on Islam); and that 'the British time, a period of bitter subjection [...] was yet for India a period of intellectual recruitment' (WC 18). However, the latter has been inadequate, Naipaul finds, to the needs of modern India (no more than a self-defeating mimicry, in fact): the book sets out to demonstrate the ubiquitousness of the Hindu psyche and attitude to life in every possible aspect of India; and simultaneously to demonstrate that this is depleted, uncreative, passive, and intellectually poor after centuries of colonial (particularly Islamic) domination.

Naipaul sees Hinduism, in a stultified but indelible fashion, looming large behind all the mimicry and disappointment of India. Its existence, together with its alleged sense of defeat and despair, explain everything that Naipaul encounters in India – these give meaning to the twice removed old world mimicry he had described in *An Area of Darkness*. These explain the novelist R. K. Narayan's novels, especially *Mr Sampath*;[1] these render the passiveness of the peasants, as Naipaul sees it, understandable; these elucidate the peculiarities (with some help from the psychologist Sudhir Kakar[2]) of Indian sexual attitudes; these explain the paucity of the arts and architecture, of technology and the sciences (described with the gleefulness of Swift describing the Royal Academy in *Gulliver's Travels*), of 'intellectual culture' generally; these illuminate the success, and deification, and failure of Gandhi (which had been seen in a more affirmative fashion in *Among the Believers*) and Gandhism, and of his disciple Vinoba Bhave; and these clarify the political débâcle of Mrs Indira Gandhi's Emergency period,[3] wherein the book is set. To find for India a discrete and essential Hindu identity, lingering in a continuous fashion from ancient times, put upon and savaged by permanently external religions like Islam, but retaining through everything its marred but still essentially Indian character – that is, briefly, the problematic and disturbing cultural essentialist project of *A Wounded Civilization*.

The problems with the asseverations of *A Wounded Civilization* are numerous. It suffers from various degrees of misinformation: its summary of the views of the Naxalites and of their ideological distance from the (in an essentially Hindu fashion) passive and ritualistic peasants was simply wrong when it was written – and continues to be so now; Naipaul's view of developments in Indian technology and the arts (especially the fine arts) in the seventies reveals deep ignorance. Naipaul's readings of events in Indian politics – especially the most immediate one when it was written, the Emergency – in terms only of some sort of Hindu psyche seems at times to be no more than an evasion of the more easily explicable vested interests and political imperatives that were involved; in fact the evocation of a Hindu psyche in that context is a redundancy. Naipaul's readings of Indian history are superficial: informed by no more than a visit to some historical sites, some textbook material, and his scepticism about popular myths; and uninformed by any attention to historical detail or historiographical understanding. The positing of the cultural essentialist notion of a pure old world Hinduism, which may be trampled underfoot, rendered passive, stultified, but which is impervious to mixture, miscegenation, hybridity – which moreover preserves itself in some shape and determines the intellectual quality of a nation – is tenuous at so many levels as a cultural and social formulation that one hardly needs to dwell on it. The idea of Hinduism is *a priori* in Naipaul's thinking: the word is thrown in wherever a pattern is discerned, and the word is not defined in theological, cultural or psychological terms with any rigour (though it appears to be efficacious in all these ways). This sort of essentialist and determinative reading is particularly problematic in as heterogeneous a context as India. The complexities of caste, class, religious community, linguistic, regional, historical, economic, political etc. alignments in India need a more complex and sociologically rigorous approach – Naipaul faithfully observes the problems and schisms that arise from these, and wilfully offers a simplistic and superficial explanation for them.

But *A Wounded Civilization* is not merely problematic in various ways, it has disturbing political antipathies and sympathies worked into it. Naipaul's dubious history places the Islamic influx as simply a very long imperialist phenomenon, vandalizing indigenous culture, and claiming allegiance to foreign authority – and in that sense, comparable to British imperialism (only rather worse). It dwells on the distant facts of Islamic conquest and the fall of Hindu Vijaynagar with all the nostalgia of someone who comes from an insular expatriate Hindu community in Trinidad, and who has predesignated India as Hindu. Naipaul refuses to see the creative impact of Islam on India, which is much more pervasive than the distant hints of conquest and war that Naipaul talks about. Naipaul fails to note

that despite communal tension, Hindu–Muslim cultural miscegenation and constructive economic coexistence has been
incomparably more fruitful in its time than any analogous
element in Indo-British contact during the British colonial
period. Naipaul suggests that the Partition, and the formation of
Pakistan, and the fraught exodus of Hindus and Muslims across
the borders, is further proof of the foreignness of Islam, and a
further betrayal of the essential Indian heritage: many would
argue that this statement is itself a betrayal of the larger number
of Muslims who continued to live in India, and within their
established heritage in that country. Naipaul's on the whole
Islamophobic views are particularly insensitive when expressed
in the context of India, where communal tensions can run high,
even though it is generally agreed (except by ultra-right political
alignments) that both communities in question are Indian and
have been so for a very long time.

Logically, but alarmingly, Naipaul's political sympathies in *A
Wounded Civilization* do turn to the ultra-right organizations
with cultural essentialist agendas. This is what Naipaul has to
say about the Shiv Sena (a regional party in the state of
Maharashtra) – I give a long quotation, the necessity for which
is, I hope, self-evident:

> The Sena 'army' is xenophobic. It says that Maharashtra, the land of
> the Marathas, is for the Maharashtrians. It has won a concession
> from the government that eighty per cent of jobs shall be held by
> Maharashtrians. The government feels that anyone who has lived in
> Bombay or Maharashtra for fifteen years ought to be considered a
> Maharashtrian. But the Sena says no: a Maharashtrian is someone
> born of Maharashtrian parents. Because of its xenophobia, its
> persecution in its early days of South Indian settlers in Bombay,
> and because of the theatricality of its leader, a failed cartoonist who
> is said to admire Hitler, the Sena is often described as 'fascist'.
>
> But this is an easy, imported word. The Shiv Sena has its own
> Indian antecedents. In this part of India, in the early, pre-Gandhi
> days of the Independence movement, there was a cult of Shivaji.
> After Independence, among the untouchables, there were mass
> conversions to Buddhism. The assertion of pride, a contracting out, a
> regrouping: it is the pattern of such movements among the
> dispossessed or humiliated.
>
> The Shiv Sena, as it is today, is of India, and it is of industrial
> Bombay. The Sena, like other recent movements in India, though

more positive than most – infinitely more positive, for instance, than the Anand Marg, The Way of Peace, now banned, which preached caste, Hindu spirituality, and power through violence, all of this mingled with ritual murder and mutilation and with homosexuality (desirable recruits were sometimes persuaded that they had been girls in previous lives) – the Sena is a great contracting out, not from India, but from a Hindu system, which, in the conditions of today, in the conditions of industrial Bombay, has at last been felt to be inadequate. It is in part a reworking of the Hindu system. Men do not accept chaos; they ceaselessly seek to remake their world; they reach out for such ideas as are accessible and fit their need. (WC 62–3)

Similar sentiments appear intermittently in *A Wounded Civilization*. The above quotation presents, to begin with, a confusing argument. Naipaul indicates a link between the Shivaji cult and the Shiv Sena, but doesn't explain the former – Shivaji was a Maharashtrian Hindu chieftain who is popularly remembered for his resistance to the Mughals. Naipaul implies that there is some link between the untouchable Buddhists and the Shiv Sena, but doesn't elucidate – it is one of antipathy. Naipaul says that the Sena 'is a great contracting out, not from India, but from the Hindu system' – but the described xenophobia is anti-Indian or anti-national, and the Sena is largely conservative Hindu in character. Naipaul sees the Sena as 'infinitely more positive' than the Anand Margis – and yet the Sena is responsible for perpetrating an incomparably larger scale of violence. (From Naipaul's point of view the Anand Margis seem to be condemned more for their alleged homosexual practices than anything else.) And Naipaul asserts that 'fascism' is an 'easy, imported word' which presumably doesn't apply – but 'fascism' is not a word fixed for perpetuity in the context of Mussolini's Italy or Nazi Germany. Fascism is a political concept: briefly and simplistically, it incorporates any attempt to define a nation or state in terms of racial, communal and cultural purity, and in that sense the Shiv Sena can be designated 'fascist'. It can be seen as positive only from a fascist (or semi-fascist) point of view. Naipaul's statement is ultimately an ideologically tilted statement: he associates the Shiv Sena with the dispossessed and the humiliated (including the untouchables or 'dalits'), with industrial Bombay, with independent India, and sees this as positive. The Shiv Sena has been (and is) uninterested in the dispossessed and humiliated and industrial workers unless these are Hindu Maharashtrians, is distant from the dalits, is implicitly anti-national in its xenophobic commitment. It probably appears to be 'positive' to Naipaul only because it perversely falls into some sort of consonance with his tenuous cultural essentialist reading of India.

Naipaul's sentiments are not the result of a flair for quixotic statement: these express real political sympathies and are the logical result of a particular development in Naipaul's thinking. I have charted out this development to some extent in this study. That Naipaul's disturbing political sympathies and antipathies in the Indian context are seriously offered is underlined by the consistency with which he has repeated them since, and by the alacrity with which these have been accepted by Hindu communal organizations in India. Before going into that, however, it is necessary to turn to his third and more voluminous book on India, *India: A Million Mutinies Now*.

India: A Million Mutinies Now (1990) is the work of a writer who looks back and reassesses his past formulations. It has an air of retrospection about it, not dissimilar to *A Turn to the South* (1985), or *The Enigma of Arrival* (1987), or, for that matter, *A Way in the World* which was to appear four years later. And as in these books, this retrospection assumes the form of a more philosophical and universalized apprehension of his experiences and of the various cultures he had observed and written about. These mature writings are an attempt to synthesize his observations about England, the Caribbean, Africa, Islamic countries, America, and India – and indeed of his personal growth through these encounters – to reach some sort of final resolution. All these books tend to be (as I have maintained earlier in this study) less culture-specific and specifically judgemental and more attuned to the broader concerns of mankind: the issue of faith, the nature of historical determinism, the spiritual needs of people, the modes of intellectual development. What devolves from these is (I repeat) a basically conservative and anti-revolutionary ideology. More importantly, the retrospection and expansion of preoccupations do not imply any withdrawal of his earlier modes of cultural appraisal and evaluation. What occurs is an attempt to present clearly a frame of thinking within which all his specific formulations (about the mimic–mimicked counterpoint in the New World, about slavery and faith in the Bible Belt of the USA, about blackness and African primitivism and violence, about the dogmatism and regressiveness of Islam, about the essential Hinduism and twice removed mimicry of India) can be coherently accommodated. *A Million Mutinies Now* falls squarely within this endeavour. It brings an ostensibly broader and more universal frame of understanding to India, which would confirm rather than invalidate any of his earlier cultural essentialist formulations.

In keeping with this approach, *A Million Mutinies Now* has a more open-ended air about it. It also has an unexpectedly reconciliatory tone: but this is clearly not actually a withdrawal of already expressed cultural essentialist views and political sympathies, rather a renewed affirmation of these. It reasserts his already familiar understanding of India in a less immediately abrasive and contentious fashion:

> There was a paradox. My continental idea of an Indian identity, with the nerves it continually exposed, would have made it hard for me to do worthwhile work in India. The caste or group stability, the more focused view, enabled them, while remaining whole to themselves, to do work – modest, improving things – rather than revolutionary things in conditions which to others might have seemed hopeless [...].
>
> Many thousands of people had worked like that over the years, without any sense of a personal drama, many millions; it had added up in the 40 years since independence to an immense national effort. The results of that effort were now noticeable. What looked sudden had been long prepared: the increased wealth showed; the new confidence of people once poor showed. One aspect of that confidence was a freeing of new particularities, new identities, which were as unsettling to Indians as the identities of caste and clan and region had been to me in 1962, when I had gone to India only as an 'Indian'. (*MMN* 8–9)

It is, of course, comforting to know that Naipaul sees definite signs of increased prosperity and confidence in India and appreciates the 'modest, improving' (rather than revolutionary) efforts of millions of people. That these efforts and their results depend ultimately on 'caste or group' stability – a stability which doesn't derive, in other words, from any nation-building effort or any dynamics of a secular community (a 'continental idea of an Indian identity') – is more or less in keeping with Naipaul's earlier reading of India's old world rootedness. Naipaul also mentions the 'freeing of new particularities, new identities' with approbation. *A Million Mutinies Now* is largely a survey of 'caste and group' stability and 'new particularities, new identities'. One finds that Naipaul's perception of 'caste and group stability' and 'new identities' is not unlinked: the latter are 'new' only in the sense that they reinvigorate (in a positive fashion, Naipaul evidently believes) what had previously been seen as stultified old world (mostly Hindu) values.

On the whole *A Million Mutinies Now* reads as an objectively presented collection of stories, more so than most of his other efforts in a similar mould. It does, however, systematically and persistently frame questions and organize the stories around notions of caste or group or particular identity. The result is better informed and more coherent than both his earlier books on India; indeed *A Million Mutinies Now* seems designed to rectify and elaborate on details in his earlier books (especially *A Wounded Civilization*). Naipaul's visit on this occasion takes him along a zigzagging route to some of the important cities from the south to the north: from Bombay (in the state of Maharashtra) and Goa, to Bangalore and Mysore (Karnataka), to Madras (Tamil Nadu), to Calcutta (West Bengal), to Lucknow (Uttar Pradesh), to Delhi (at that time a Union Territory), to Chandigarh (also then a Union Territory), to Amritsar (Punjab), and finally to Srinagar (Kashmir). By and large the people Naipaul meets in each city represent some sort of local movement or group or are identified by Naipaul as such. So the visit to Bombay is marked primarily by stories of Shiv Sena leaders and activists, a Dalit (Untouchable) leader and writer, people on the fringe of the Bombay film industry, Hindu and Muslim gangsters and entrepreneurs. The former Portuguese colony of Goa recalls the New World for Naipaul. In Bangalore Naipaul meets some progressive Brahmins, particularly scientists, politicians, executives. In Mysore his most memorable encounter is with a Hindu priest connected to the erstwhile Hindu royal household of Mysore. The visit to Madras centres primarily around those who are involved in the anti-Brahminical and anti-religious but caste-based politics of the Dravidian movement. In Calcutta he goes into the history of the ultra-left Naxalite movement with former Naxalites and their sympathizers. In Lucknow he talks to a range of Muslims, commoners and ex-royalty. In Delhi he interviews certain conservative and liberal editors and publishers of women's magazines, which allows Naipaul to dwell on the situation of Indian women. In Chandigarh and Amritsar Naipaul investigates the phenomenon of the Sikh secessionist movement and terrorism – he meets associates of the Sikh secessionist and terrorist leader Bhrindan-wale (who died during the military Operation Bluestar, which flushed out the terrorists from the Golden Temple), and also some victims of terrorist violence. And finally, in Srinagar, Naipaul associates with Kashmiri Muslims – this final section has more of a personal and nostalgic touch to it, since it describes meetings with persons he had lived with during his first visit to India in 1962.

So, as Naipaul moves from west to east to west and from south to north in *A Million Mutinies Now*, India seems to fragment into different groups and identities, according to: religious community (Hindu, Muslim, Jain, Sikh, Buddhist); region (Maharashtrian, Tamil, Bengali, Punjabi, etc.); religion overlapping with region (Lucknavi Muslim, Kashmiri Muslim; Maharashtrian Hindu, Tamil Hindu, Mysore Hindu, etc.); caste (upper, middle, lower); ideological persuasion (Shiv Sena, Dravidian, Congress, Naxalite, etc.); caste overlapping with ideological persuasion overlapping with religion (dalit Maharashtrian Buddhist, lower caste Tamil Dravidian, etc.); occupation (executives, scientists, politicians, priests, gangsters, etc.); occupation overlapping with all these (Karnataki Brahmin scientist, Naxalite lecturer, Tamil Brahmin executive, Maharashtrian Jain entrepreneur, etc.); and all overlapping with class and economic standing (poor, prosperous, holding a certain social status, etc.); and finally, all these fraught with gender issues. The picture is complex; and the complexity is authentic to the enormous heterogeneity of India. Naipaul faithfully captures this heterogeneity. He does so, and this is where his cultural essentialist thinking comes through, with a penchant for seeing old world values as playing a determinative regenerative role with regard to modern developments and preoccupations. As a case in point, his comments on the Brahmin scientists he met in Bangalore may be cited. His discussion with two of them lead, for instance, to reflections such as these:

My thoughts, as I had driven down from Goa, through the untidy but energetic towns, full of the signs of growth, and then through the well-tilled fields at harvest time, had been of the Indian and, more specifically, Hindu awakening. If Subramaniam was right, there was a hidden irony in that awakening: that the group or caste who had contributed so much to that awakening should now find itself under threat. (*MMN* 161)

Unsurprisingly, for Naipaul Indian 'awakening' (in this context the development of science and technology) is equivalent to Hindu awakening. The fact that he met scientists of Brahmin backgrounds doesn't immediately suggest that such a background was uniquely and perhaps unfairly well-situated to pursue education and a certain kind of intellectual development; to Naipaul this appears to be to the particular credit of Brahmins. He doesn't consider the cultivation of science as a supersession and levelling out of conservative Brahminical values; he sees this as a development and regeneration of Brahmins as such. And to him the 'threat' to Brahmins doesn't appear to be a natural condition of any awakening, it seems to be ironical. Many other such observations can be cited from *A Million Mutinies Now*.

Having covered his field, as it were, and demonstrated in an impressive fashion the variegated colours and enormity of Indian society and culture – having, in other words, apprehended the fragmentations and fissures in India – he tries in the final chapter to comprehend it all in an overarching formulation.

In the 130 years or so since the Mutiny [. . .] the idea of freedom has gone everywhere in India. Independence was worked for by people more or less at the top; the freedom it brought has worked its way down. People everywhere have ideas now of who they are and what they owe themselves. The process quickened with the economic development that came after independence; what was hidden in 1962, or not easy to see, what perhaps was only in a state of becoming, has become clearer. The liberation of spirit that has come to India could not come as release alone. In India, with its layer below layer of distress and cruelty, it had to come as disturbance. It had to come as rage and revolt. India was now a country of a million little mutinies.

A million mutinies, supported by twenty kinds of group excess, sectarian excess, religious excess, regional excess: the beginnings of self-awareness, it would seem, the beginnings of an intellectual life, already negated by old anarchy and disorder. But there was in India now what didn't exist 200 years before: a central will, a central intellect, a national idea. The Indian Union was greater than the sum of its parts; and many of the movements of excess strengthened the Indian state, defining it as the source of law and civility and reasonableness. (*MMN* 517–18)

The form of the idea is not too far from Jawaharlal Nehru's understanding of India's 'unity in diversity'. But it is different: it essentially maintains (as it must if Naipaul is to adhere to his cultural essentialist perception of India) that all the excess and violence is a necessary part of India's unity and development, that some of these are indeed necessary for India's 'awakening' – that, in fact, in the current condition of India anything goes. It does not seem to occur to him that what he sees as a 'million little mutinies' could coalesce into something larger which might (if not assessed adequately and in time) distort and pervert the delicate balance of the 'Indian Union'. Naipaul's notion of a million mutinies in India could be seen as another way of continuing to accommodate what had been most disturbing and unwelcome in *A Wounded Civilization*.

Though *A Million Mutinies Now* admittedly differs from *A Wounded Civilization* in assuming a more affirmative tone about India's present and future, in its basic approach to India it is as essentialist and politically worrying as the earlier book. The more disturbing aspects of *A Wounded Civilization* outlined above have been consistently maintained by Naipaul in his various articles and interviews about India which have appeared since he wrote *A Million Mutinies Now*. The nineties in India have been witness to a particularly strong wave of Hindu communal politics. It could be seen to have taken off with the destruction of Babri Masjid in Ayodhya in December 1989 to establish a temple to the Hindu god Rama, ostensibly because the latter was born there; there had allegedly been a temple there before which was destroyed and replaced by the mosque by Emperor Babur (the first Mughal emperor). The historical basis for the mythological claim to that land is flimsy and tenuous; the historical circumstances of the latter claim are also far from clear. Several excellent historical and sociological works about the dubiousness of the Hindu communalists' claims and evidence[4] (which Naipaul is clearly unaware of) have been available from

93

shortly after the incident. The initiation, build-up and culmination of what is now known as the Ayodhya movement was largely sponsored and organized by a political party, the Bharatiya Janata Party (BJP) (whose members hoped to fulfil political aspirations by playing the Hindu communal card and espousing a Hindu communalist agenda) and certain ultra-Hindu organizations which are affiliated to this party, like the Vishwa Hindu Parishad (VHP) and the Rashtriya Swayamsevak Sangh (RSS). The destruction of Babri Masjid led to communal violence between Hindus and Muslims on a nationwide scale unprecedented since the Partition. Throughout the nineties the relationship between the two religious communities has deteriorated, jingoism and Hindu communalism have flourished, the BJP has gradually and steadily consolidated its position (with some assistance from the corrupt practices and incompetence of the other national parties) – and it has recently culminated in the BJP leading a coalition to form the government. Naipaul has been a constant supporter of the rise of Hindu communal politics in India, which can (despite Naipaul's objections) be unproblematically and accurately described as semi-fascist and fundamentalist.

Naipaul has reiterated his superficial and schematic view of Indian history (an Islamic invasion from approximately AD 1000 which has vandalized a self-contained essentially Hindu India, followed by an intellectually debilitating Muslim imperialism and an intellectually regenerative British imperialism, the main victims in all of which have been Hindu Indians), and his vision of progress through a constant rediscovery of this 'true' history (wherein the 'million mutinies' uncomplicatedly become for Naipaul a positive Hindu movement). These views have been reasserted in a controversial interview with Dileep Padgaonkar which appeared in *The Times of India* (18 July 1993), in an article entitled 'A Million Mutinies' which appeared in *India Today* (18 August 1997) on the occasion of fifty years of India's independence, and most recently in another interview with Rahul Singh in *The Times of India* (23/24 January 1998). In all of these, he has restated his simplistic views of history, with as little attention to detail, current research, and historiographical thinking as was evident in *A Wounded Civilization*. His references to Indian historians is unthinkingly dismissive – he absurdly believes they are all Marxist (and therefore must be flawed), and usually cites Romila Thapar's book as a good example (the book in question is the Pelican *History of India*, vol. 1, 1966, itself a sketchy and popular historical account by an eminent historian). Apart from an unwarranted conviction in the 'truth' of his view of Indian history, the only significant aspect of this view is that it is very close to that of pioneers of modern Hindu communalism. It is, for example, very similar to the view of Indian history to be found in V. D. Savarkar's *Hindutva* (1942) (literally 'Hinduness'), in which Savarkar, one of the founders of the VHP, called for a racially, culturally, and nationally pure Hindu India.[5]

Naipaul's views coincide with those of fundamentalist and semi-fascist Hindu communalists beyond this. Naipaul has actively expressed his support of Hindu communalist movements and organizations which have resulted in or caused large-scale violence and bloodshed. In the 18 July 1993 *Times of India* interview with Padgaonkar, Naipaul came out in favour of the destruction of the Babri Masjid, and described the communal violence as the symptom of the regeneration of a historically slighted Hindu India which has remained insulted and humiliated for a thousand years – 'a movement from below', 'a mighty creative process'. When the Shiv Sena and the BJP won the elections in Maharashtra in 1995, Naipaul described this as a 'good sign' and reportedly said 'you must be sympathetic to a movement that is laying claim to the land. You cannot dismiss it as fascist' – according to a report in the *Indian Express* (2 April 1995). In the 23/24 January 1998 *Times of India* interview with Rahul Singh, he makes similar points again about the Ayodhya issue and the rise of the BJP, albeit in a more circumspect fashion:

> I don't think the people of India have been able to come to terms with that wrecking [of the Islamic invasion around AD 1000]. I don't think they understand what really happened. It's too painful. And I think this BJP movement and that masjid business is part of a new sense of history, a new idea of what happened. It might be misguided. It might be wrong to misuse it politically, but I think it is part of a historical process. And to abuse it as Fascist is to fail to understand why it finds an answer in so many hearts in India.

(Odd last sentence: fascism had seemed the answer to many in Europe in the 1930s.) This coincidence of views with Hindu communalists has also meant that Naipaul has constantly exacerbated the Indian Muslim's sense of insecurity, and aired anti-Islamic sentiments. That also is all too coherent with his writings about Islam – but I have gone into that already.

On the whole, Naipaul's writings on India have some merits. They demonstrate a certain dedication on the part of the writer, who persistently tries to delve deeper into an unwieldy social and cultural formation. In them, Naipaul characteristically displays his talent for close observation and ability to assimilate carefully what he sees before him. And in bringing these qualities to bear on India over a sufficient period of time and with patience he does convey something of the complexities and diversities of India in an impressive fashion – especially in *A Million Mutinies Now*. On the other hand, Naipaul's writings on India also demonstrate that the kind of observed surface truth that he leans towards can lead to deeply tenuous and unstudied perceptions. His penchant for cultural essentialist analysis and evaluation results in particularly disturbing political connotations in the Indian context. To summarize simplistically:

(a) Naipaul has offered theoretical support (in the shape of a distorted view of history, a tenuous notion of India as essentially Hindu, and certain abstract platitudes about historical process) to fundamentalist and semi-fascist Hindu communal ideologies in India, and has seen as positive that which is patently detrimental to the happiness and security of the Indian people now and in the future. He protests that he is interested only in cultural ideas and historical progressions – if that is so, his failure to see the pragmatic implications of expressing sympathy for xenophobia and communalist organizations is irresponsible.

(b) He has consequently condoned the large-scale violence perpetrated at the behest of Hindu communalist organizations, and directed primarily against Muslims. He has contributed thereby to the sense of insecurity of more than 110 million legitimate and rooted citizens of India – the Muslims. By implication, this sense of insecurity could extend to other smaller minorities too.

Naipaul's writings on India have appeared at regular intervals throughout a long and accomplished career, and my survey does, I hope, convey not only his specific views on India but also the general tenor of his preoccupations and reflections. Naipaul has engaged with a wide variety of interlinked issues and contexts: the issues range from personal history to the historical determination of culture and society; from colonization to the constitution of post-colonial states; from the complexities of specific racial groups, religious communities, and nationalities, to the broader concerns of human spiritual needs, intellectual life, political ideology; from fiction to reality and from fantasy to truth. Most of Naipaul's critics[6] have maintained that what ultimately underlies this broad canvas and even transcends it is his quality as a writer; that irrespective of whether one agrees or disagrees with his cultural evaluations and asseverations, whether one sympathizes with his views about the world or with his attempts to find his place in the world, the literary art of Naipaul has been of an unvaryingly high quality and renders everything he has written worthy of note. Naipaul is ultimately memorable not merely for his thoughts and ideas (these are often questionable), his critics maintain, but because he is a good, perhaps great, *writer* of books. This brings us back to the point with which I began the present study: Naipaul's self-consciousness as a writer of books, his sense of the physical tangibility of the book, and of the closure of the book. Arguably Naipaul has always maintained this consciousness of being a writer of books – it has meant that his attention to the language, form, style of his books displays a consistent attention to completion. Naipaul has always worried about the perfection of the book, irrespective of what it may state, and the results are aesthetically pleasing. In that sense Naipaul's books have been invariably readable and satisfying, as his critics have customarily maintained.

The separation between evaluations of how well Naipaul has written and what he has written implicit in such critical sentiments, however, need not be accepted. Judging from his critical views (expressed in so many of his books, essays and interviews), Naipaul himself would be reluctant to go along with such a separation. It could justifiably be maintained, for instance, that if Naipaul has used predominantly realistic narratives in his novels it is because he is persuaded that there is always a reality to be authenticated, a truth to be discerned, and there are universal human criteria to be employed in engaging with different societies and contexts. His use of distanciation techniques, his attempts at placing himself objectively, his endeavour occasionally to efface the writer – and all the formal nuances consequent on these – are part of this project to discern and express human truths, authentic features and universal evaluative criteria. The very motivation behind his self-exposure to different cultures and contexts, and the confidence with which he does this, is grounded in this conviction. Ideological commitments (such as being anti-revolutionary, being a cultural essentialist, being a seeker after authenticity, being conservative, even being spiritually attuned) derive from his convictions, and the stylistic nuances of his writings are conditional upon these – they permit him to be lyrical, angry, scathing, jokey, and so forth. If to evaluate Naipaul's writings aesthetically is to mean anything more than commending him for his indubitably sound grasp of the English language, it would have to explore the conjunction of what he has written and how he has written about it. The critical industry which has grown around Naipaul's writings will, I expect, continue to do that.

Notes

CHAPTER 1.   INTRODUCTION

1. Rahul Singh, 'Magic Realism Has Encouraged People to Hide from the Truth' (interview with Naipaul), *The Times of India* (New Delhi), 24 January 1998, p. 12.
2. See, for instance, the section entitled 'The Early Short Stories', in Selwyn R. Cudjoe, *V. S. Naipaul: A Materialist Reading* (Amherst: University of Massachusetts Press, 1988), 20–8.

CHAPTER 2.   THE FIRST FOUR BOOKS

1. According to Steven Vertovec, *Hindu Trinidad: Religion, Ethnicity and Socio-Economic Change* (London and Basingstoke: Macmillan, 1992):

    > The system of magic popularly known as *obeah* is common to Trinidadians of all religions and ethnic groups. Originally drawn from West African *obayifo* (witchcraft) systems, these magical beliefs, acts, and symbols have been combined or made interchangeable with those of North India, known as *ojha*. *Obeahmen* or *ojhamen* (both also called 'seer-men') may be African or Indian, and of any religion (however, they tend to be Spiritual Baptists or Shangoists in the first case, Hindus in the second); their clients are equally mixed. (pp. 216–17)

    This information is not only illuminating in the context of the novel, but also interesting in view of Naipaul's sentiments about racially mixed Caribbean societies discussed later.
2. For a useful discussion of Naipaul's use of the calypso see ch. 1. in John Thieme, *The Web of Tradition: Uses of Allusion in V. S. Naipaul's Fiction* (London: Hansib, 1988), ch. 1.
3. For instance, Keith Warner, *The Trinidadian Calypso* (London: Heinemann, 1982), chs. 1–3.
4. In the 1994 BBC *Face to Face* interview with Jeremy Isaacs, for instance, and in 'Prologue to an Autobiography' (FC 73–81).

CHAPTER 6. FILLING GAPS

1. By 'conservative' I mean a definite set of ideas (rather than simply the opposite of radical) – such as those outlined in Roger Scruton, *The Meaning of Conservatism* (London: Macmillan, 1984).
2. Naipaul's 'plea for snobbery' in the essay 'What's Wrong With Being a Snob?' (*Saturday Evening Post*, 3 June 1967, pp. 12, 18) is worth recalling here – it is reprinted in Robert D. Hamner (ed.), *Critical Perspectives on V. S. Naipaul*, 34–8.

CHAPTER 7. WRITING ABOUT ISLAM

1. As enunciated in Ivan Illich, *Deschooling Society* (London: Calder and Boyars, 1971).
2. David Dabydeen, 'In God's Aeroplane', *Independent Saturday Magazine*, 2 May 1998, pp. 10–11.

CHAPTER 8. WRITING ABOUT INDIA AND CONCLUSION

1. R. K. Narayan, *Mr Sampath* (London: Eyre & Spottiswood, 1949). Naipaul's reading of this is to the point; there is a distinct Hindu spiritualist vein in many of Narayan's novels.
2. Sudhir Kakar has since presented his views on this subject in book form – *Intimate Relations: Exploring Indian Sexuality* (Harmondsworth: Penguin, 1990).
3. In 1974 there was growing unrest in India about inflation and corruption within the ruling Congress Party. Charges of campaign malpractice were proved against Prime Minister Indira Gandhi on 12 June 1975. Emergency was declared by the President at the instance of the Prime Minister on 26 June 1975, whereby all civil rights were suspended, restrictions were imposed on the press, and the armed forces were put on special alert. Most opposition party leaders were arrested. Indira Gandhi called off Emergency Rule in 1977, and the Congress Party lost the subsequent elections to the Janata Party.
4. These include Anand Patwardhan's documentary film *Ram ki Nam* (1992) and *Pita, Putra aur Dharm Yudh* (1991); S. Gopal (ed.), *Anatomy of a Conflict* (New Delhi: Penguin India, 1991); Ashish Nandy et al., *Creating a Nationality: The Ramjanmabhumi Movement and Fear of the Self* (Delhi: Oxford University Press, 1997); and Tapan Basu et al., *Khaki Shorts, Saffron Flags* (New Delhi: Orient Longman, 1993).

5. In *Hindutva* (1923; Poona: Lokasamgraha Press, 1942), V. D. Savarkar presents Indian national identities as based on an homogeneous Hindu culture which was destroyed by Muslim invasion – and therefore calls for an official description of India as Hindu, where Hindu is defined as an overlapping of race (*jati*), culture (*sanskriti*), and nation (*rashtra*) (p. 74).

6. Most recently in Fawzia Mustafa, *V. S. Naipaul*, 219.

Select Bibliography

BOOKS BY V. S. NAIPAUL

The Mystic Masseur (London, 1957; Harmondsworth, 1964; New York, 1984).

The Suffrage of Elvira (London, 1958; Harmondsworth, 1969; New York, 1985).

Miguel Street (London, 1959; Harmondsworth, 1971; New York, 1984).

A House for Mr Biswas (London, 1961; Harmondsworth, 1969; New York, 1984).

The Middle Passage: Impressions of Five Societies – British, French and Dutch – in the West Indies and South America (London, 1962; Harmondsworth, 1969; New York, 1981).

Mr Stone and the Knights Companion (London, 1963; Harmondsworth, 1969; New York, 1985).

An Area of Darkness (London, 1964; Harmondsworth, 1968; New York, 1981).

The Mimic Men (London, 1967; Harmondsworth, 1969; New York, 1985).

A Flag on the Island (London, 1967; Harmondsworth, 1969).

The Loss of El Dorado: A History (London, 1969; New York, 1970; Harmondsworth, 1973; New York, 1984).

In a Free State (London, 1971; Harmondsworth, 1973; New York, 1984).

The Overcrowded Barracoon and Other Articles (London, 1972; New York, 1973; Harmondsworth, 1976; New York, 1984).

Guerrillas (London, 1975; New York, 1975; Harmondsworth, 1976; New York, 1980).

India: A Wounded Civilization (New York, 1977; Harmondsworth, 1979; New York, 1977).

A Bend in the River (New York, 1979; Harmondsworth, 1980; New York, 1980).

'The Return of Eva Perón' with 'The Killings in Trinidad' (New York, 1980; Harmondsworth, 1981; New York, 1981).

A Congo Diary (Los Angeles, 1980).

Among the Believers: An Islamic Journey (New York, 1981; Harmondsworth, 1982; New York, 1982).

Finding the Centre: Two Narratives (New York, 1984; Harmondsworth,
1985; New York, 1986).

The Enigma of Arrival: A Novel (New York, 1987; Harmondsworth, 1987;
New York, 1988).

A Turn in the South (New York, 1989; London, 1989).

India: A Million Mutinies Now (London, 1990).

A Way in the World: A Sequence (New York, 1994; London, 1994).

Beyond Belief: Islamic Excursions Among the Converted Peoples (London, 1998).

OTHER WRITINGS BY NAIPAUL

The following is a selection from the numerous uncollected articles and
reviews which Naipaul has written. For a comprehensive list of his
writing prior to 1975 – and especially of his many reviews for the *New
Statesman* – the bibliography in Robert D. Hamner (ed.), *Critical
Perspectives on Naipaul* (Washington DC, 1977), may be consulted. This
also reprints selected articles and interviews by Naipaul. Kelvin Jarvis's
V. S. Naipaul: A Selective Bibliography with Annotations, 1957–1987
(Metuchen, NJ, 1989) should also be consulted, as should his recent
update entitled 'V. S. Naipaul: A Bibliographical Update, 1987–1994', in
Ariel, 26 (October 1995), 71–85. It may be worth checking the V. S.
Naipaul archives web-site.

'Trollope in the West Indies', *Listener*, 15 March 1962, p. 461.

'India's Cast-Off Revolution', *Sunday Times* (London), 25 August 1963,
p. 17.

'Critics and Criticism', *Bim*, 10:38 (January–June 1964), 74–7.

'The Documentary Heresy', *20th Century*, 173 (Winter 1964–5), 107–8.

'Without A Dog's Chance', *New York Review of Books*, 18 May 1972, pp.
29–31.

Foreword to *The Adventures of Gurudeva and Other Stories*, by Seepersad
Naipaul (London, 1976).

'A Note on a Borrowing by Conrad', *New York Review of Books*, 16
December, 1982, pp. 37–8.

'Writing *A House for Mr Biswas*', *New York Review of Books*, 24 November
1983, pp. 22–3.

'An Island Betrayed', *Harper's*, 268:1606 (March 1984), 62–72.

'Among the Republicans', *New York Review of Books*, 25 October 1984, pp.
5, 8, 10, 12, 14–17.

'On Being a Writer', *New York Review of Books*, 23 April 1987, p. 7.

'A Plea for Rationality', in I. J. Bahadur Singh (ed.), *Indians in the*

Caribbean (New Delhi 1987), 17–30.

'Our Universal Civilization', *New York Review of Books*, 31 January 1991, pp. 22–5.

'Argentina: Living With Cruelty', *New York Review of Books*, 30 January 1992, pp. 13–18.

'The End of Peronism?', *New York Review of Books*, 13 February 1992, pp. 47–53.

'A Million Mutinies', *India Today*, 18 August 1997, pp. 36–7, 39.

INTERVIEWS

Applewhite, James, 'A Trip with V. S. Naipaul', *Raritan*, 10:1 (Summer 1990), 48–54.

Bingham, Nigel, 'The Novelist V. S. Naipaul Talks About His Childhood', *Listener*, 7 September 1972, pp. 306–7.

Hardwick, Elizabeth, 'Meeting V. S. Naipaul', *New York Review of Books*, 13 May 1979, pp. 1, 36.

Harris, Michael, 'Naipaul on Campus: Sending out a Plea for Rationality', *Tapia*, 29 June 1975, p. 2.

Hussein, Aamer, 'Delivering the Truth: An Interview with V. S. Naipaul', *Times Literary Supplement*, 2 September 1994, pp. 3–4.

Isaacs, Jeremy, 'Face to Face: V. S. Naipaul', broadcast on BBC2, 16 May 1994.

Kazin, Alfred, 'V. S. Naipaul, Novelist as Thinker', *New York Review of Books*, 1 May 1977, pp. 20–1.

Medwick, Cathleen, 'Life, Literature and Politics: An Interview With V. S. Naipaul', *Vogue*, August 1981, pp. 129–30.

Michener, Charles, 'The Dark Visions of V. S. Naipaul', *Newsweek*, 16 December 1981, pp. 104–17.

Mukherjee, Bharati and Boyers, Robert, 'A Conversation with V. S. Naipaul', *Salmangundi*, 54 (181), 4–22.

Padgaonkar, Dileep, 'An Area of Awakening', *Sunday Times of India*, 18 July 1993, pp. 10–11.

'Religion Is Often a Smokescreen for Political Oppression', *The Times of India*, 1 May 1998, p. 13.

Roach, Eric, 'Fame a Short-Lived Cycle, says Vidia', *Trinidad Guardian*, 4 January 1972, pp. 1–2.

Rowe-Evans, Adrian, 'Interview with V. S. Naipaul', *Transition* (Ghana), 40 (1971), 56–62.

Singh, Rahul, 'Poor People, Distress are Hard to Bear: Naipaul', *The Times of India*, 23 January 1998, pp. 1, 10, 11.

Walcott, Derek, 'Interview with V. S. Naipaul', *Sunday Guardian* (Trinidad), 7 March 1965, pp. 5, 7.

BOOKS ABOUT NAIPAUL AND HIS WORKS

Boxhill, Anthony, *V. S. Naipaul's Fiction: In Quest of the Enemy* (Fredericton, New Brunswick, 1983).

Cudjoe, Selwyn, *V. S. Naipaul: A Materialist Reading* (Amherst, 1988).

Gurr, Andrew, *Writers in Exile: The Creative Use of Home in Modern Literature* (Atlantic Highlands, NJ, 1981).

Hamner, Robert D., *V. S. Naipaul* (New York, 1973).

Hamner, Robert, D., (ed.), *Critical Perspectives on V. S. Naipaul* (Washington, DC, 1977).

Hassan, Dolly Zulakha, *V. S. Naipaul and the West Indies* (New York, 1989).

Hughes, Peter, *V. S. Naipaul* (London, 1988).

Jarvis, Kelvin, *V. S. Naipaul: A Selective Bibliography with Annotations, 1957–1987* (Metuchen, NJ, 1989).

Kelly, Richard, *V. S. Naipaul* (New York, 1989).

King, Bruce, *V. S. Naipaul* (Basingstoke and London, 1993).

Mason, Nondita, *The Fiction of V. S. Naipaul* (Calcutta, 1986).

Morris, Robert K., *Paradoxes of Order: Some Perspectives on the Fiction of V. S. Naipaul* (Columbia, 1975).

Mustafa, Fawzia, *V. S. Naipaul* (Cambridge, 1995).

Nightingale, Peggy, *Journey Through Darkness: The Writing of V. S. Naipaul* (St Lucia, 1987).

Nixon, Rob, *London Calling: V. S. Naipaul: Postcolonial Mandarin* (New York and London, 1992).

Rai, Sudha, *V. S. Naipaul* (New Delhi, 1982).

Rao, K. I. Madhusudana, *Contrary Awareness: A Critical Study of the Novels of V. S. Naipaul* (Madras, 1982).

Theroux, Paul, *V. S. Naipaul: An Introduction to his Work* (London, 1972).

Thieme, John, *The Web of Tradition: Uses of Allusion in V. S. Naipaul's Fiction* (London, 1988).

Walsh, William, *V. S. Naipaul* (London, 1973).

Weiss, Timothy, *On the Margins: The Art of Exile in V. S. Naipaul* (Amherst, 1992).

White, Landeg, *V. S. Naipaul* (London, 1975).

RECENT ARTICLES ABOUT NAIPAUL AND HIS WORKS

Most of the preceding books and bibliographical sources cite important articles published prior to the nineties. The following is a list of articles that have appeared in the nineties.

Berger, Roger A., 'Writing Without a Future: Colonial Nostalgia in V. S.

Naipaul's *A Bend in the River'*, *Essays in Literature*, 22 (Spring 1995), 144–56.

Bilgrami, Akeel, 'Cry the Beloved Subcontinent', *New Republic*, 10 June 1991, pp. 30–4.

Brice-Finch, Jacqueline, 'V. S. Naipaul's Dystopic Vision in *Guerrillas'*, *Studies in Literary Imagination*, 26 (Fall 1993), 33–43.

Dabydeen, David, 'In God's Aeroplane', *Independent Saturday Magazine*, 2 May 1998, pp. 10–11.

Dayan, Joan, 'Gothic Naipaul', *Transition*, 59 (1993), 158–70.

Gorra, Michael, 'Naipaul or Rushdie', *Southwest Review*, Summer 1991, pp. 374–89.

Gourevitch, Philip, 'Naipaul's World', *Commentary*, 98 (August 1994), 27–31.

Fraser, Robert, 'Fathers and Sons: Mr. Biswas and Mr. Soyinka', *Journal of Commonwealth Literature*, 28:2 (1993), 93–107.

Haywood, Helen, 'Tradition, Innovation, and Representation of England in V. S. Naipaul's *The Enigma of Arrival'*, *Journal of Commonwealth Literature*, 32:2 (1997), 51–65.

Huggan, Graham, 'V. S. Naipaul and the Political Correctness Debate', *College Literature*, 21 (October 1994), 200–6.

Irwin, Robert, 'He Knew He Was Right', *Guardian*, 2 May 1998, p. 8.

Jarvis, Kelvin, 'V. S. Naipaul: A Bibliographical Update', *Ariel*, 26 (October 1995), 71–85.

Langran, Phillip, 'V. S. Naipaul: A Question of Detachment', *Journal of Commonwealth Literature*, 25:1 (1990), 132–41.

Nathan, Melina, 'V. S. Naipaul's *The Enigma of Arrival'*, *New Voices* (Trinidad), 18:35/6 (March–September 1990), 43–67.

Nixon, Rob, 'Preparations for Travel: the Naipaul Brothers' Conradian Atavism', *Research in African Literatures*, 22 (Summer 1991), 177–90.

O'Brien, Michael, 'An Intelligent Mechanism: Naipaul on the South', *The Mississippi Quarterly*, 43 (Winter 89/90), 77–83.

Pritchard, William H., 'Naipaul's Written World', *Hudson Review*, 47 (Winter 1995), 587–96.

Rampersad, Arnold, 'V. S. Naipaul: Turning in the South', *Raritan*, 10:1 (Summer 1990), 24–39.

Roy, Ashish, 'Race and the Figures of History in Naipaul's *An Area of Darkness'*, *Critique*, 32 (Summer 1991), 235–57.

Walker, W. John, 'Unsettling the Sign: V. S. Naipaul's *The Enigma of Arrival'*, *Journal of Commonwealth Literature*, 32:2 (1997), 67–84.

Ware, Tracy, 'V. S. Naipaul's The Return of Eva Perón and the Loss of "True Wonder"', *Ariel*, 24 (April 1993), 101–14.

Weiss, Timothy, 'V. S. Naipaul's "fin de siècle": "The Enigma of Arrival" and "A Way in the World"', *Ariel*, 27 (July 1996), 107–24.

Wise, Christopher, 'The Garden Trampled: or, the Liquidation of African Culture in V. S. Naipaul's *A Bend in the River'*, *College Literature*, 23 (October 1996), 58–72.

Index

Recent and Forthcoming Titles in the New Series of

WRITERS AND THEIR WORK

WRITERS AND THEIR WORK
RECENT & FORTHCOMING TITLES

RECENT & FORTHCOMING TITLES